BARRED FROM THE BAR

A History of Women in the Legal Profession

by Hedda Garza

Women Then—Women Now

Franklin Watts

A Division of Grolier Publishing

New York London Hong Kong Sydney
Danbury, Connecticut

This book is dedicated to the New York City
legal team of Michael and Debby Smith, and Los Angeles
public defender Michael Fischman.
Among the last of the "People's Lawyers," they practice
in the self-centered 1990s with the morality and
loving care of the 1960s still intact.

Photographs copyright ©: New York Public Library Picture
Collection: pp. 18, 24; Jay Mallin, Library of Congress:
pp. 23, 38, 51; Library of Congress: p. 76; Sophia Smith Collection
(Women's History Archives): p. 90; The Bettmann Archive: p. 98;
UPI/Bettmann: pp. 114, 181; Reuters/Bettmann: p. 172;
Supreme Court Historical Society: pp. 128, 130; AP/Wide
World Photos: pp. 137, 161, 175, 177.

Library of Congress Cataloging–in–Publication Data

Garza, Hedda.
Barred from the Bar: a history of women in the legal
profession / by Hedda Garza.
p.   cm. — (Women then—women now)
Includes bibliographical references and index.
ISBN 0–531–11265–9 (lib bdg.)—ISBN 0–531–15795–4 (pbk.)
1. Women lawyers—United States—History—Juvenile literature.
2. Sex discrimination against women—United States—History
—Juvenile literature.   I. Title. II. Series.
KF299.W6G37   1996
349.73'082—dc20
[347.30082]   95–49391 CIP AC

BARRED FROM THE BAR

On August 23, 1995, Hedda Garza, the author of this book, died in Glens Falls, New York. She was 66 years old.

Outspoken and charismatic, Hedda was an impassioned writer and political activist who devoted her life to the cause of social justice. As if obsessed with making freedom and equality a reality, she tirelessly engaged the critical issues of our day, outraged by injustice and committed to the belief that the world could be changed for the better—even if she would have to change it herself!

For years, Hedda fought the battles in the streets. Later she spent more time lecturing and writing than she did marching, but whatever form her protest took, it was always powerfully persuasive. She was a humanist, intent on doing her part to end racial and gender discrimination, war, and the oppression of the poor. In everything she said and did, she was brutally honest, and she demanded that our political leaders set the same example. She was motivated in equal parts by anger and compassion, and she inspired everyone who came in contact with her both to reflect and, just as importantly, to act.

I consider myself very fortunate to have served as Hedda's editor and publisher since 1985, but also simply to have known her. It is difficult to accept that someone so full of life is no longer living. The struggles she made her own endure. Thankfully, her work and, for some, the memory of her endure as well.

John Selfridge
V.P. & Publisher
Grolier Children's Publishing

CONTENTS

INTRODUCTION

In 1994 and 1995, television audiences watched in fascination as Marcia Clark, Los Angeles deputy district attorney, argued forcefully and capably during the trial of celebrity O. J. Simpson, accused of a brutal double murder. Clark had served as prosecutor in a number of important cases, winning all of them.

Although Simpson's so-called "dream team" of defense lawyers was all-male, no one seemed to think it odd that a woman was playing the lead role in presenting the prosecution's case. Few realized that until very recently, women lawyers and judges were rarely seen in courtrooms. Now women lawyers work as public defenders, law firm associates (sometimes partners), district attorneys, and in private practice. Two women, Sandra Day O'Connor and Ruth Bader Ginsburg, are associate justices of the highest court in the land, the United States Supreme Court.

When Judge Ginsburg accepted President Bill Clinton's nomination on June 14, 1993, she thanked her mother and remembered the past deprivations of women: "I pray that I may be all that she would have been had she lived in an age when women could aspire and achieve and daughters are cherished as much as sons," she told the assembled reporters.[1]

Most of those who heard the speech believed Judge Ginsburg was talking about long-gone attitudes. Even some who knew about the struggles by women to gain entry into the legal profession thought the battle had finally been won. Over a hundred years, after all, had passed since Myra Bradwell's application for a lawyer's license had been turned down by the Illinois Supreme Court:

> When the Legislature gave to this court the power of granting licenses to practice law, it was not with the slightest expectation that this privilege would be extended equally to men and women. . . . This we are not yet prepared to hold.[2]

Bradwell had passed the bar examination with flying colors, was the publisher of a leading legal newspaper, the wife of a prominent Cook County judge, and had many friends in high places. If she could be prevented from practicing law, there seemed no possibility that others could succeed.

The judges had made it clear that Bradwell was not their personal target. They believed that barring women from law practice should be a universal rule, and expressed concern over whether "the hot strifes of the Bar, in the presence of the public . . . would not tend to destroy the deference and delicacy with which it is the pride of our ruder sex to treat her."[3]

Bradwell appealed to the United States Supreme Court in what has been called the first sex discrimination case to be heard by the highest court in the land (*Bradwell* v. *Illinois*, 1873). It delayed its negative decision for more than three years. Meanwhile, Bradwell's action provoked fresh outbursts of male indignation over women's attempt to enter the professions.

At a conference of the American Medical Association, for example, Dr. Alfred Stillé took the floor to give a passionate speech against all women who dared to knock at the doors of the all-male medical and legal worlds. "The women question in relation to medicine," he said,

> is only one of the forms in which the *pestis muliebris* [female plague] vexes the world. In other shapes it attacks the bar, wriggles into the jury box and clearly means to mount upon the bench. . . . [4]

Stillé's fears must have seemed groundless to many. The *Bradwell* decision by the Illinois Supreme Court should have gone a long way toward allaying the fears of those who wanted to keep women "in their place." Women had few legal rights, not even the right to vote. The Fifteenth Amendment to the United States Constitution, ratified in 1866, allowed African-American males to vote; women, black or white, were not included in the new suffrage amendment.

Those who tried to break down the barriers to equality were subjected to ridicule and rejection from every quarter. After delaying their decision until 1873, not only did seven of the eight Supreme Court justices uphold the Illinois Supreme Court decision, but in his written opinion Justice Joseph Bradley went even further than his Illinois colleagues:

> The natural and proper timidity and delicacy which belongs to the female sex evidently unfits it for many of the occupations of civil life. . . . The paramount destiny and mission of woman are to fulfill the noble and benign offices of wife and mother. This is the law of the Creator. . . . [5]

Most judges, the watchdogs of the legal profession, agreed wholeheartedly with Justice Bradley's position and guarded the doors to their forbidden realm with ardor. Not until a century later, in the 1970s, would Stillé's nightmare vision of women lawyers, judges, and jurists have even the slightest basis in reality.

Under Myra Bradwell's leadership, a few brave women continued to "attack the bar" and finally won the right to practice law. But they were scarcely able to earn a living at their hard-won profession. It wasn't until the 1970s, *fifty years* after women were finally permitted to vote, that the roadblocks to the legal profession appeared finally to be crumbling.

It *seemed* that way, but there were also many signs that the ghosts of Supreme Court Justice Bradley and others of his ilk still haunted the world of law. On October 3, 1994, *The New York Times* featured an article describing Marcia Clark's "transformation" after a mock jury in Phoenix, Arizona, in August "gave Ms. Clark a stinging rebuke." Their critique had nothing to do with her obvious knowledge and legal talents. Apparently Clark had not shown "the natural and proper timidity and delicacy which belongs to the female sex." The article reported that Ms. Clark "has clearly been told to get with the program: warmer, fuzzier, more juror friendly."

To accomplish this, Clark apparently headed for the nearest beauty parlor and clothing store. She emerged with "shorter, better-kept hair that framed her face, warmer and lighter-colored dresses with softer fabrics, more jewelry." When she met with the press, "magically, her voice had warmed up. She smiled often, and incandescently. She laughed, even giggled, repeatedly. *She rolled her eyes, cocked her head and shrugged her shoulders.*" (Italics added) Instead of terse "no comments," Clark spoke about her harried new life, her shopping trips, her children. According to the *Times*:

a jury consultant from Miami, said domestic themes like grocery shopping and children were crucial tools in the makeover, and motherization, of Marcia Clark. Since both male and female jurors are put off by tough women lawyers, . . . the old Marcia Clark was in "a no-woman's land."[6]

Imagine the jokes and consternation if Robert L. Shapiro, Simpson's chief defense attorney, had been advised to giggle repeatedly, roll his eyes, cock his head, and shrug his shoulders, or had shown up at a press conference in soft silk shirts with a fluffy new toupee framing his face! But according to the news media, the one comment Shapiro made when he was asked what he thought of his opposing counsel was "Great legs!"

There are many other signs, too, that the fight for women's equality is far from over. The victories that started to occur in the 1970s were rolled back sharply in the 1980s (see Chapter Six). The "no-woman's land" of the "old Marcia Clark" still existed, ready to drag women back to their "paramount destiny" of "the noble and benign offices of wife and mother," as per "the law of the Creator," rather than permit them to continue to "attack the bar" and "mount upon the bench."

If these fears were realistic, there would be only two choices for women: they could give up and go home, or they could become an army of thousands of modern-day Myra Bradwells taking on the most powerful force in the nation—the law.

1

WITH A FOOT
ON THEIR NECKS

*I ask no favors for my sex. I surrender not our
claim to equality. All I ask of our brethren is that
they will take their feet from off our necks and
permit us to stand upright on the ground which
God has designed us to occupy.*

—*Sarah Grimké, abolitionist leader* [1]

It was no less than amazing that Myra Bradwell even considered becoming a lawyer. For almost a hundred years after the American Revolution, not one single woman had been permitted to practice law.[2] Only a few worked as physicians,[3] perhaps because women had always been assigned the caretaker role—nursing sick family members and even neighbors. But law was another matter. It was, after all, the center of *power*.

Court decisions not only determined the guilt or innocence of those accused of crimes. The courts ruled on marriage relations, property rights, and civil disputes—all decided by lawyers, judges, and juries, who were always male.

The laws interpreted by the legal establishment were passed by the ruling bodies of the nation, from Congress to the state legislatures, all of them composed of men, most of them lawyers. Their legislation reflected and reinforced the prevailing attitudes toward women.

Women did not *lose* their legal status in the newborn United States. *They had never had any rights under the law in the first place!*

Throughout most of recorded history, in fact, women had been viewed as the "other," the inferior of men.[4] The famous words of Thomas Jefferson's Declaration of Independence that "all men are created equal" meant just that. Mixing flattery with insult, Jefferson had also said that American women would be "too wise to wrinkle their foreheads with politics." As president, Jefferson wrote that women's education should be limited to "the amusements of life . . . dancing, drawing, and music."[5]

Until 1920, except for a very brief period in New Jersey when, between 1776 and 1807, "all free inhabitants" who owned property could vote, state constitutions barred women from voting or holding office. Without the ability to select those who made the laws, they could do little to change the oppressive laws themselves. Although single women were banned from public activities such as voting, jury service, and public office, so long as they did not marry they could own and manage their own property, keep their own earnings, sign contracts, sue and be sued, and will their possessions to anyone of their choice. They were automatically deprived of *all* of these rights on the day they said "I do." At that point "coverture" laws applied, under which the woman became "one" with her husband, his powerless "other" half.[6]

Not surprisingly, many women from wealthy families remained single, not wanting to lose all of their control and power as individuals. In those days, a husband had the right to commit his wife to an insane asylum without even a legal hearing to determine her sanity. Divorce was not a real option for women either. In the few states where divorces were legal, the husband automatically retained custody of all property, *including any children.*

As one historian has expressed it, "Women were civilly dead and without political rights."[7] Once they were married, their life often became a cycle of pregnancy, births, and drudgery. Even their bodies no longer belonged to them. If a woman refused to give in to her husband's sexual demands, he could institute divorce proceedings or beat her, *all with the law on his side*. Contraception was prohibited. Although condoms had been used since the sixteenth century and were mass-produced in the 1840s, the law banned their sale. Again, it was the man's choice alone if he wished to buy some on the sly. Not until the 1930s, when the Great Depression made it almost impossible to feed large families, was birth control legalized in most states.

The law also viewed rape as a violation of the rights of *men*, who, after all, controlled their wives' and daughters' bodies! Behind all of these decrees was the issue of property rights. If a woman became pregnant after being raped, there was no way to establish the fatherhood of the offspring. The offspring of another man could later make claims on the husband's property!

The attitudes were derived from the Bible and English common law. The inferior status of women was justified by the Bible story of the "original sin" of Eve in the Garden of Eden. As England's laws evolved, the idea of husband and wife as "one" came to mean that the wife sublimated her entire self to her mate.

Eventually these rules were collected and documented in Blackstone's *Commentaries*, required reading for all students of the law.[8] Blackstone was merely recording decisions made centuries earlier. The earliest and most revered philosophers—Roger Bacon, Thomas Aquinas, Albertus Magnus, all of them important religious figures as well—warned about the evildoings of witches, women in league with the devil. This fear-mongering paved the way for the Inquisition of the fifteenth, sixteenth, and seventeenth centuries, with women the favorite targets.[9]

The chapter titles of *Malleus Maleficarum*, the instruction manual for the witch-hunters, read like a prescription for future coverture laws: "Evil Began with Eve" and "Never Allow Women to Exercise Power."[10]

Given these long-enduring traditions and laws, it is amazing that women protested at all. For one thing, there were certain seeming advantages to the laws of coverture. Women traded freedom for financial support and protection. Under the male-dominant system known as patriarchy, men were required to support their families. If the man died, his widow had the legal right to one third of her husband's real estate for the rest of her life.

A husband was responsible for "a crime committed by his wife in his presence, without any evidence of any complicity or knowledge on his part."[11] This, of course, placed husbands in an even more dominant position. If they could be charged with a crime committed by their wives, they had all the more reason to constantly monitor their wives' behavior!

Many people incorrectly believe that women accepted their status until long after the American Revolution. But in March 1776, as the Founding Fathers drafted the Constitution, John Adams received a letter from his wife, Abigail Adams, warning him that if "particular care and attention are not paid to the ladies, we are determined to foment a rebellion, and will not hold ourselves bound to obey the laws in which we have no voice of representation."[12]

Reportedly, John said, "I cannot but laugh."[13] Perhaps he laughed because the truth was that Abigail and other women of the time had little ability to "foment a rebellion." Living isolated from one another, with no organizations, women who daydreamed about even modest legal rights must have been unaware that there were others with similar forbidden ideas. Moreover, women had few vehicles for protest other than the written word. Although ninety percent of the colonial men could read and write, less than half of the women were literate. In

Abigail Adams warned her husband, John Adams, that if
women's rights were not recognized, women were "determined
to foment a rebellion, and will not hold ourselves bound to obey
the laws in which we have no voice of representation."

most colonies, girls either were not educated at all or their education was inferior to that provided for boys.

There were only a tiny handful of men who supported equal rights for women. In 1775, Tom Paine, the famed pamphleteer whose writings helped to convince thousands of men and women of the necessity of freedom from England, wrote an article on the legal status of women, describing them as

> robbed of freedom and will by the laws, the slaves of opinion, which rules them with absolute sway and construes the slightest appearances into guilt; surrounded on all sides by judges, who are at once tyrants and their seducers. . . . Who does not feel for the tender sex?[14]

Apparently the Founding Fathers paid no attention to Paine's attitudes toward women. The U.S. Constitution ignored three groups that desperately needed relief—African slaves, Native Americans, and women.

The lives of most "tender" women were filled with hardship. In Philadelphia alone, 4,000 women and children worked long hours in their shabby homes spinning cloth for local merchants under the "putting out" (piecework) system. Many single or widowed women ran small shops or at-home businesses brewing beer or baking breads. In the cities, thousands of homeless people wandered the streets begging.[15]

Most history books say little about the role of women during the American Revolution, but for all women, even the most sheltered, the war brought not only new hardships but new responsibilities. Women got together in Daughters of Liberty groups. Meeting in one another's homes, they formed sewing clubs to make their own clothes in order to boycott British imports. But they also involved themselves in far less "ladylike" activities.

In 1777, Abigail Adams again wrote to her husband, this time describing an action carried out by a group of about a hundred women or more against a "wealthy, stingy merchant" who raised his coffee prices when tea was being boycotted. With talk accomplishing nothing, the women

> marched down to the warehouse, and demanded the keys, which he refused to deliver. Upon which one of them seized him by his neck and tossed him into the cart . . . he delivered the keys when they tipped up the cart and discharged him; then opened the warehouse, hoisted out the coffee themselves, put it into the trunks and drove off. . . . A large concourse of men stood amazed, silent spectators of the whole transaction.[16]

Most women were not as daring. But during the long drawn-out war on American soil, 25,000 people—almost 1 percent of the population of less than 3 million—lost their lives, and many women became "deputy husbands." They took over the responsibility of running farms, handling finances, and raising children alone as their husbands went off to war, sometimes never to return.

When independence was finally won, nothing would ever be the same. No doubt many women had gained not only new skills but the confidence that went with them. Disappointed that their new republic continued to deprive them of voting rights, property rights, and a public role, a handful of women circulated the writings of early feminists.

These pioneers concentrated at first on pressuring the state legislatures for educational facilities for women. Clearly, women could not dream of even partial equality, let alone professional careers, if they were deprived of schooling. In their drive to obtain the right to education, they had to buck a myth prevalent in the period that women's brains were smaller than men's and therefore they were intellectually inferior. The experts of the day, all male, claimed that any effort on the part of women to try their hands at intellectual pursuits could only lead to mental breakdown.

Judith Sargent Murray, born in 1751, wrote angry essays challenging these theories. Murray, the daughter of a wealthy Massachusetts shipowner, had been only modestly educated during her childhood, while her brother had been carefully groomed to attend Harvard University. Secretly, she read and studied her brother's books, perhaps feeling more deprived and angrier each day.

Murray's collected essays, *On the Equality of the Sexes*, were written during the Revolution but not published until 1790. Murray, obviously talking about her own family situation, agitated against the unequal education of boys and girls.[17]

In the twenty years after the Revolution, dozens of female academies were opened, teaching a modified version of the basic academic subjects taught in the schools for boys, along with homemaking courses. Almost all of the students came from middle-class and wealthy homes. The literacy gap between the sexes began to close, except in the South.

Woman educational reformers tried various tactics. Perhaps to reassure the male establishment or perhaps because they believed their own words, some endorsed sexual inequality in education.[18] But a few forged ahead in open defiance of traditional beliefs. In 1819, Emma Willard petitioned the New York State legislature for an endowment for a girls' school. Willard protested that "the taste of men, whatever it might happen to be, has been made into a standard for the formation of the female character." She urged the legislators to recognize that "we too are primary existences . . . not the satellites of men."[19] Willard won the support of Governor De Witt Clinton for her project. Unfortunately, it was verbal support without financial backing.

Refusing to accept defeat, Willard struggled for more than a year, raising money. In 1821, she founded the Troy Female Seminary, the first state-chartered institution for the education of girls, with a broader curriculum than ever had existed before. Lucy Stone, who would go on to be a leading women's rights advocate and abolitionist (opponent of slavery), was one of several outstanding graduates of Willard's school.

One woman refused to accept any compromise on full equality for her sex. Frances Wright joined Robert Owen's utopian colony of New Harmony, located in rural Indiana, in 1828. In the group's newspaper, she argued that *men's* lives were damaged by the degradation of women. By accepting the false ideas of female inferiority, she said, they would live out their lives without a true companion. Wright also took to the lecture circuit, calling for free education for all workers. Similar arguments would not be heard again for more than a century. Until then, changes came slowly, usually only because of economic necessity.

Westward expansion in the 1830s and 1840s, for instance, created a need for labor in the new territories, and women began to do "men's" jobs. As the rules for women's roles broke down, it became easier to demand equality on other scores, like education.

Early in that period, Oberlin, which would become the first women's college, began its existence. It was founded as a ladies' seminary in 1833 by the leaders of a student sit-in at the Lane Seminary in Ohio when blacks and women were not permitted to enroll. It then gradually evolved into a college. From its first term, Oberlin admitted African American, as well as white, women. Lucy Stone referred to the opening of Oberlin as "the gray dawn of our morning."

Stone was undoubtedly disappointed. The early administration of the college expressed firm agreement with the leading male educators of the day that motherhood was the "highest calling" for women. They believed

Frances Wright argued that men's lives
were damaged by the degradation of women.
She also called for free education for all workers.

Lucy Stone, suffragist

that "If women became lawyers, ministers, physicians, lecturers, politicians or any sort of public character the home would suffer from neglect."[22] Stone was asked to write a commencement speech but refused the assignment when she was told it would be read by a male.[23]

As middle and upper-class women became educated, they longed to do more than stay home embroidering and entertaining. Looking for a role in public life, many joined a growing number of societies to aid widows, orphans, the poor, and the mentally ill. Some joined religious organizations and went abroad as missionaries.

They were soon to hear about the terrible lives of working women in the textile mills of New England. By 1817, factories sprang up to meet the demands of a growing population. In the mills, girls barely in their teens worked fourteen to sixteen hours a day, earning only a fourth of men's wages.

These working women had little patience for lady-like behavior in the face of such crushing conditions. In Lowell, Massachusetts, working women formed the first major women's union, the Lowell Female Labor Reform Association, led from 1845 to 1846 by a young woman named Sarah Bagley. When the mill owners tried to fire leaders of the union for speaking out on their conditions, Bagley made a fearless speech unmatched in its emotion and eloquence by any of the better-educated reformers of the day:

> What! Deprive us, after working thirteen hours, of the poor privilege of finding fault—of saying our lot is a hard one! . . . We will make the name of him who dares to act stink with every wind, from all points of the compass. His name shall be a by-word among all laboring men, and he shall be hissed in the streets, and in all the cities of this widespread republic; for our name is legion though our oppression be great.[24]

25

The Lowell women went door to door, circulating petitions demanding a ten-hour day to the Massachusetts legislature. Perhaps believing that women would not dare appear before their august body, the legislators invited them to present their petitions in person. The women did not win their demands.

On the other hand, a few middle-class women reformers had their eyes opened to the existence of "sisters" whose lives were completely different from their own. They decided to help the working women in the struggle for reforms.

The issue that evoked the most response from women was slavery. It was impossible to hide, unlike the isolated textile mills. Although the slave trade had been legally abolished in Great Britain and the United States in 1808, merchants in the port cities and slave exporters in several states were unwilling to relinquish the huge profits they received from the transport and sale of human beings. In the southern United States, there were willing and ready customers, anxious to expand their plantations. In the United States alone, there were about two million African slaves by 1830. That number doubled in the next thirty-five years.

In 1831, newspapers carried the story of Nat Turner's defeated slave revolt, and in Boston, William Lloyd Garrison's antislavery weekly newspaper, *The Liberator*, was founded. With only a few women present, antislavery men, called abolitionists, founded the American Anti-Slavery Society in Philadelphia in 1833. Not permitted to join the organization, twenty women got together at the end of the conference and formed their own Philadelphia Female Anti-Slavery Society. Chapters were organized in New York and several New England towns.

In May 1837 the first National Female Anti-Slavery Society convention took place in New York City. They turned down offers of male help because "they found they had *minds* of their own."[25] (Italics added.) Their founding platform called for struggle against both slavery and the inequality of women. They denounced not just slavery but *all* race prejudice. They called for the racial integration of churches and schools. Certainly because of their firm stand on racism, they were joined by several black women, including little-known figures like Sara Parker Remond, Charlotte Forten, Sarah Mapps Douglass, Letetia Still, Harriet and Sarah Forten, some of whom were elected as leaders.

The struggle over equal participation of women in the abolitionist movement continued. In the spring of 1838, when women were permitted to participate equally with men at the New England Anti-Slavery Convention, some men resigned and later formed the male-only Massachusetts Abolition Society. There were similar splits elsewhere. Perhaps rejection by some of the men in the abolitionist groups added fuel to the fire of women's demands for equal rights. Perhaps they expected men who opposed slavery to be in the forefront of the freedom struggle for *all* people.

Eventually the American Anti-Slavery Society voted to accept women as full members. Most of the men had come to realize that unity could make the difference between success and failure. Frederick Douglass, himself a fugitive from slavery, held unquestioned authority in the abolitionist movement. He spoke out forcefully, praising the contribution of women to the abolitionist struggle.[26]

Two sisters from a South Carolina slaveholding family, Sarah and Angelina Grimké, began speaking against slavery in public in 1836, and other women followed their lead. Abolitionist women made speeches everywhere they went—in their sewing circles, charitable groups, and literary societies.

The Grimké sisters were the first to link the struggle for the emancipation of the slaves to the struggle for women's equality. In *An Appeal to the Christian Women of the Southern States*, Angelina Grimké urged southern women to revolt against patriarchy and male property rights by rising up against slavery and even freeing their own slaves. Her sister Sarah dared to attack the churches for using the Bible to justify the subordination of women. On Eve's responsibility for Original Sin, she shocked many by commenting that "Adam's ready acquiescence with his wife's proposal" raised questions about "that superiority in strength of mind" attributed to men.[27]

Such strong talk on women's rights made some of the abolitionist men nervous. Asked to tone down her antislavery speeches, Angelina Grimké refused, insisting,

> If we surrender the right to speak in public this year, we must surrender the right to petition next year, and the right to write the year after, and so on. What then can woman do for the slave, when she herself is under the feet of man and shamed into silence.[28]

Women were playing an increasingly important role in a rapidly growing American Anti-Slavery Society. Fearing women's participation in civic and religious affairs, many religious leaders attacked "the dangers which at present seem to threaten the female character with widespread and permanent injury."[29]

Proslavery men behaved more violently toward the women in the abolitionist movement than toward the men. Even rational congressmen seemed to lose their reason when they confronted women in action who would not be kept "in their place." In 1834, for example, a group of women in the American Anti-Slavery Society initiated a very successful petition campaign to Congress against the admission of additional slave states. Going door to door in several towns, the women were often abused by jeering crowds of rowdies. The U.S. House of Representatives quickly passed the Pinckney Gag Rule, forbidding the presentation of any and all petitions to Congress!

Abigail Adams would have been proud of her seventy-year-old son, John Quincy Adams. During the debate on the gag rule, the Massachusetts congressman and former U.S. president called the "departure of women from the duties of the domestic circle" a "virtue of the highest order."[30]

As women fought for freedom for the slaves and equal rights for themselves, a countermovement came to the fore, called the "Cult of Domesticity" or the "Cult of True Womanhood." An outpouring of writings and speeches on women's "special" role insisted that women were "separate but equal," the guardians of the home. Those who joined the women's rights and abolitionist movements, the new preachers of domesticity insisted, were doomed to face despondency and mental disease.

A virtual war of words took place, with many newspapers and magazines pushing the "cause" of domesticity. The advocates of women's rights relied on abolitionist papers to publish their views. Voting rights were seldom discussed. Movement women seemed far more concerned about their legal rights. Only gradually did they come to realize that without the vote it would be difficult to pressure legislators to change the laws.

The earliest campaigns for equal rights for women centered on the issue of property rights. In 1836, six women signed a petition to the New York State legislature asking for a Married Woman's Property Law to end coverture rules on property and wages. Ernestine Rose, a recently arrived Polish Jew, drafted the proposed legislation. She worked for weeks just to collect five precious signatures. Some of the ladies said the gentlemen would laugh at them, she later commented; others, that they had rights enough. The legislature stalled until 1848 and then passed the new law. Over the next decades, other states passed similar legislation, but the repressive laws on divorce, female incarceration for "insanity," and other vital issues remained intact.

Far more daring and seldom mentioned in history books was a legislative petition campaign in Massachusetts in 1840 by abolitionist women to repeal a so-called mis-cegenation law, forbidding sexual relations and marriages between the races. The women pointed out that the law presumably protected white women from black men but had not a word to say about black women raped by white men, a far more common occurrence. A black woman abolitionist, Lydia Maria Child, initiated the campaign, and several other black women became active in it.

It took special courage for these Massachusetts women to stand in the town squares and go door to door circulating their legislative petitions. They collected more than 9,000 signatures, two thirds of them obtained from other women. Called harlots and promiscuous women, the petitioners were accused of sexual misbe-havior. Year after year for a decade they presented their petitions to the legislature, not achieving victory until almost ten years later.[31]

During those years dozens of women were learn-ing the ins and outs of the law—from the legal lan-guage of proposals for legislation to the mechanisms of getting bills passed. By 1840, the American anti-slavery movement included a quarter of a million peo-ple. Despite male resistance, most of the 1,350 local societies endorsed the demands for women's equal-ity. Fifty-three delegates were elected to attend a World Anti-Slavery Convention in London, England, in June to discuss ways of ending the world slave trade. But on opening day the question of the pres-ence of women delegates became the main issue on the agenda.

The British delegates insisted that all women be excluded from the proceedings. They then proposed a compromise. Women could watch silently from a cur-tained-off area. Wendell Phillips, a leading white male American delegate, angrily introduced a countermo-tion that the women be seated as full delegates.

As expected, the British won overwhelmingly. According to the later writings of a leading woman in the American movement, Elizabeth Cady Stanton, two men—William Lloyd Garrison and Nathaniel P. Rogers—protested by joining the women in the gallery. Stanton failed to mention another male protestor, black abolitionist Charles Redmond.

The women delegates excluded from the London antislavery convention began talking about holding a convention of their own, devoted to the issue of women's rights. Eight years later, in 1848, they succeeded. In a small Methodist church in the town of Seneca Falls, New York, 300 people, including about forty men, most of them abolitionists, drafted a Declaration of Principles on women's equality with an appended list of grievances. Along with demanding the right for women to vote and to keep their own property and wages, the delegates demanded women's right to a college education, equal opportunity in employment, and entry into the professions of medicine and law.

At the time of the Seneca Falls convention, seventeen-year-old Myra Bradwell was attending an exclusive female seminary. It is likely that with the other young women students she pored over the reports of the historic events in upstate New York, reading the widely publicized statement of the delegates complaining that man had

> endeavored, in every way that he could, to destroy her confidence in her own powers, to lessen her self-respect and to make her willing to lead a dependent and abject life. . . .[32]

Perhaps young Myra Bradwell decided then and there that she would never "lead a dependent and abject life," that she would fight for equality for herself and all women.

31

2

PIONEERS: ATTACKING
THE BAR

. . . she must have known the court would decide
against her, unless she either supposed that they were
likely to be influenced by personal solicitation and
clamor, or else that they were all gone crazy.

—*Editorial in* The Nation, *April 1873, on*
Myra Bradwell's appeal to the Supreme Court
to permit her to practice law [1]

It is probably true that Myra Bradwell was not at all surprised in 1873 when the United States Supreme Court, strictly on the basis of her sex, refused her a license to practice law. The reaction of one of the more liberal publications in the United States, *The Nation* (see above), probably did not shock her either. Yet Bradwell willingly subjected herself to a virtual landslide of opposition and ridicule, from enraged newspaper editorials and cruel political cartoons to catcalls on the street.

Bradwell's life story makes it obvious that America's "first" woman lawyer had a goal that went far beyond her own personal ambitions. There is much evidence that her fight for admission to the bar was a deliberate test case (*Bradwell* v. *Illinois*, 1873) to open the door to other women lawyers and broaden the struggle for women's rights.

Actually, Bradwell was not the first woman admitted to the bar, although she was given that title in 1890. Margaret Brent, who acted as the administrator for the estate of Maryland's governor Leonard Calvert in the 1640s, is often referred to as the first (and only) woman attorney on the American continent before the American Revolution. Then, for over 200 years there is no record of a practicing woman attorney![2]

Bradwell's first success came as she lay dying with cancer. Her husband, James Bradwell, secretly convinced the Illinois Supreme Court to admit her to the state bar, antedating her admission to 1869, the date of her original application. Two years later the United States Supreme Court followed suit. Then, just months before Bradwell's death in 1894, the Illinois Bar Association called her "the pioneer woman lawyer" in recognition of the fact that she had waged a battle that battered down the doors for all those who followed her.

Like many of the women struggling for equality in the nineteenth century, Bradwell was raised by parents who supported the antislavery cause. Eben and Abigail Willey Colby were descendants of pioneer settlers of Boston. Bradwell, born on February 12, 1831, was the youngest of five Colby children. In 1843, five years before the Seneca Falls convention, the Colby family moved close to Elgin, Illinois. They became friendly with the family of Elijah Lovejoy, the publisher of an abolitionist newspaper who had been gunned down in 1837 by a mob of proslavery men. The parlor of the Colby home was the scene of many discussions on the pressing issues of the day: the struggle against slavery and the fight for women's equality.

With so few educational options for young women, Myra was sent to live with a married sister in Wisconsin, where she attended a typical "female seminary." Her "higher" education consisted of a year's preparation for a teaching career at another seminary in her hometown.

Bradwell received a good basic education along with instruction in the tenets of the Cult of Domesticity or True Womanhood, including religious devotion, submissiveness to male authority, and sole dedication to the task of building a good marriage and rearing virtuous children. Talented young women like Myra Colby were told not to worry about careers for themselves, except perhaps as grade school teachers, but to use their assets to help their future husbands advance in the world.

A year after she started teaching at the Elgin Female Seminary, Myra Colby broke the rules. She fell in love with James Bolesworth Bradwell, an apprentice law student working as a laborer to support himself. The Colby family disapproved of her poverty-stricken suitor. Myra's big brother Frank Colby, armed with a shotgun, ordered James Bradwell to stay away from his sister. Defying all of the conventions of the day, Myra Colby and James Bradwell eloped in 1852.

The young couple opened a private school in Memphis, Tennessee, where James Bradwell was admitted to the bar. Two years later, Myra was pregnant and the Bradwells moved to Chicago. James Bradwell won admission to the Illinois bar, and apparently the family patched things up. In 1855, when James Bradwell opened his first law office, his new law partner was none other than Myra's gun-toting big brother Frank.

Although Myra and James Bradwell raised four children, only two surviving, she was often seen in her husband's law office. Friends and family were told that Myra wanted to "work side by side and think side by side with her husband," but actually she was all the while studying for the bar examination. By the time the Civil War broke out in 1861, James Bradwell had been elected to a judgeship and Myra Bradwell, now referred to as Mrs. Judge Bradwell, gave most of her time to women's organizations involved in providing aid to wounded Union soldiers.

Not long after the end of the war, on October 3, 1868, the first issue of the weekly *Chicago Legal News* appeared, announcing that it would cover "legal information, general news, new and important decisions . . . and other matters useful to the practicing lawyer or man of business."[3] Myra Bradwell's name appeared on the masthead as publisher, editor, and business manager. She had quietly obtained permission from the Illinois legislature to run the business under her own name.

Within a few years, the *Chicago Legal News* enjoyed the highest circulation of any legal publication in the nation. Myra Bradwell provided information unavailable elsewhere. Attorneys had often felt handicapped by the long lag times between the passage and publication of new legislation. Bradwell convinced the Illinois legislature to provide her with copies of all legislation as each session ended. She then made similar agreements with other state legislatures and even the federal courts and Supreme Court. Regular reading of the *Chicago Legal News* enabled lawyers to go into court with full knowledge of the latest laws as well as court decisions in important cases. A consummate businesswoman, Bradwell invested some of her profits in a highly successful printing and binding plant.

If Bradwell had let matters stand at that, she would have been famous as one of a very few successful woman entrepreneurs in the nation, but she had much more ambitious goals. The *Chicago Legal News* ran regular columns on the need to reform the law profession by expelling incompetent, dishonest, and alcoholic lawyers, often involved in jury bribing. In another regular column called "Law Relating to Women," Bradwell argued eloquently for thoroughgoing reform of laws pertaining to divorce, child custody, and the rights of the mentally ill. Women's rights organizations published newsletters and pamphlets also agitating for equal rights for women. Male legislators rarely looked at the pamphlets, but they could not avoid seeing Bradwell's pieces.

Myra Bradwell's interest in women entering the legal profession was evident in every issue of her publication. She ran enthusiastic items on the handful of talented women practicing law in small towns after apprenticing with sympathetic male attorneys. None of these women had applied for state licensing, knowing that they would be refused.

Then, in June 1869, Bradwell gave full coverage to an important test case for women's entry into the legal profession. A twenty-three-year-old schoolteacher, Arabella Babb Mansfield, applied for admission to the Iowa bar before Judge Francis Springer, an outspoken believer in women's equality. Mansfield had graduated with honors from Iowa Wesleyan College, served an apprenticeship at her brother's law firm, and then achieved a high score on the bar examination.[4]

Although Iowa law limited bar membership to white males, Judge Springer found a loophole in the legal code and admitted Mansfield. The following year the state legislature officially changed the language of the restrictive law. Mansfield had won her point, but although she was the first woman to win bar admission in the entire country, she never practiced law.[5]

Certainly Mansfield's victory influenced Myra Bradwell. If Iowa could allow women to practice law, why not Illinois? On August 2, 1869, Myra Bradwell sailed through the Illinois bar examination and applied to the Illinois Supreme Court for her license, touching off a legal struggle that lasted for the next four years.

Setting an example for all who followed her, Bradwell refused to give up. She prepared her now famous appeal to the United States Supreme Court, but she did far more than that. In the pages of the *Chicago Legal News*, Bradwell launched a campaign for the admission of women to law schools and the bar in every state in the Union.

The majority of lawyers still prepared for their bar examinations as apprentices, but slowly university education became the norm. After the Civil War, government-supported land-grant colleges such as the University of California, the University of Michigan, and Syracuse University admitted a few women. The St. Louis Law School was the first law school to accept women. Bradwell applauded these advances in the *Chicago Legal News*. She also reminded her readers that women still could not practice without a court-granted license.

Bradwell focused first on her home state, where two women, Alta Hullett and Ada Kepley, were attempting to "attack the bar." Hulett had completed an apprenticeship, passed the bar examination and, as expected, had been turned down by the Illinois Supreme Court. Through a "leak" from one of her many readers, Myra Bradwell learned that one of the judges on the examining committee had commented that Hulett answered legal questions "much more readily than the four gentlemen who were examined with her and have since been admitted to the bar."[6]

Ada Kepley had graduated with honors from the University of Chicago Law School, one of the two females in the institution's first class, which also included two black men. In 1870, Bradwell announced in her paper that Kepley had been denied the right to practice in Illinois.

It took Kepley a decade to gain admission to the Illinois bar. Writing about her experiences, she said:

It seems I was the first woman to graduate from a law school in the world, and in addition, Amer-

Myra Bradwell campaigned for the acceptance
of women lawyers throughout the United States.

ica, which boasted to the rest of the world to be "the land of the free and home of the brave," gave no freedom to her women. . . . I work as hard as a man, I earn money like a man . . . I am robbed as a woman. I have no voice in anything or in saying how my money, which I have earned, shall be spent. . . . Women might be cooks, wash women, floor scrubbers and do any sort of menial labor at that time, but they were barred from the so-called learned professions.[7]

Bradwell had many allies among her readers. One Illinois trial court judge, willing to jeopardize his own standing, offered to admit Kepley to practice before his court even without a state license. Bradwell turned him down. She had another, more ambitious plan in mind.

Rather than wait while the Supreme Court decided on her own case, and perhaps because an unfavorable decision was expected, Bradwell sat down with Alta Hulett and drafted the first equal employment opportunity bill for women. The proposed law stated that "No person shall be precluded or debarred from any occupation, profession, or employment (except military) on account of sex."[8]

Most of the men serving in the Illinois legislature were lawyers, the vast majority of them readers of the *Chicago Legal News*, and some of them friends of the Bradwells. Under a steady hammering of logical prose in her paper and in person, Bradwell miraculously managed to convince a majority to vote for her proposed law. Women in Illinois were legally free to pursue whatever occupation they chose.

Alta Hulett promptly reapplied for admission. On the day that Hulett stood before the bar to receive her hard-won license at the age of nineteen, one of the justices publicly declared, "If you were my daughter, I would disinherit you!"[9]

At that point Myra Bradwell could easily have reapplied and received her Illinois license, but by then it was clear that she was more interested in spreading the equal opportunity victory to other states. Throughout the 1870s, in the pages of the *Chicago Legal News* and in person, Bradwell became the champion of women attempting to enter colleges, pass the bar, and win the right to practice law. When courts would not budge, she was there to draft legislation and push it through to passage.

There was no active women's movement to help her. The unified abolitionist–women's rights movement that had existed before the Civil War ended in a rancorous split in 1869, leaving a divided movement concentrating on winning suffrage for women.[10] That split affected not only Myra Bradwell but also other women striving for equal opportunity.

After the Civil War, Susan B. Anthony, Frederick Douglass, Elizabeth Cady Stanton, and a few other abolitionist leaders had founded the Equal Rights Association to continue the fight for the civil rights of the newly freed slaves. Many had assumed that if former slaves were given the right to vote, women would also win suffrage. The Fifteenth Amendment shattered such illusions by stating that the "right of citizens of the United States to vote shall not be denied or abridged by the United States or any State on *account of race, color, or previous condition of servitude.*" (Italics added.)

The word sex or gender was nowhere to be seen! Women would continue to be denied the right to vote.

Susan B. Anthony and Elizabeth Cady Stanton announced in the pages of their newspaper *The Revolution* that they would work to defeat the Fifteenth Amendment. At the Equal Rights Association convention in May 1869 in New York City, the issue tore apart the long-standing coalition between abolitionists fighting racism and women struggling for equal rights, creating a breach that would do irreparable damage to both causes for decades to come. It would not be until the Civil Rights Movement, almost a century later, that antiracists and women's rights groups would again join forces. Frederick Douglass, urging continued work for the women's vote, pleaded with the assembled delegates to support the partial victory. Lucy Stone supported him.

During hours of heated debate, tempers flared. Elizabeth Cady Stanton made racist remarks about "Sambo" and the enfranchisement of "Africans, Chinese, and all the ignorant foreigners the moment they touch our shores." Susan B. Anthony added to the furor by saying, "I will cut off this right arm of mine before I will ever work for or demand the ballot for the Negro and not the woman."[11]

A split was unavoidable.[12] Anthony and Stanton formed the National Woman Suffrage Association, banning men from membership. Stone and others issued a call for a convention in Cleveland in November 1869 to form their own organization. Susan B. Anthony was shocked to see Myra Bradwell's name on the list of those supporting the Stone group.[13] In the pages of the *Chicago Legal News* Bradwell had editorialized angrily against the denial of suffrage to women. Yet here she was aligning herself with the "moderates"!

At the Cleveland convention the "moderates" created the American Woman Suffrage Association (AWSA) and decided to work for the right to vote on a state-by-state basis and steer clear of other women's rights issues. Bradwell organized the first woman suffrage convention in the Midwest in Chicago early in 1869, winning endorsement of woman's suffrage from many area judges and attorneys. Endorsements were one thing but votes in state legislatures quite another. The newly created Illinois State Suffrage Association could not persuade the state legislature to grant women the vote. The same situation prevailed all over the nation.

Throughout the 1870s, Bradwell took on many causes simultaneously. During the presidential election of 1872, when Susan B. Anthony led sixteen women in Rochester, New York, to the polls to attempt to vote, the Grant administration decided to prosecute her. Despite her differences with Anthony, Bradwell's *Chicago Legal News* was the only legal periodical defending her.

Bradwell also continued her work to change centuries-old divorce and custody laws. By 1871, largely through her tireless efforts, new legislation existed in several states requiring the consent of both parents in custody decisions.

Most of Bradwell's energies in the 1870s, however, were spent on the exhausting task of helping women gain law school and bar admission on a state-by-state basis. Although the legislation she and Hulett had won in Illinois certainly meant that Bradwell could now successfully apply for her law license, she did not try again. Two cases Bradwell took up illustrated all the male prejudice women faced at every turn.

The first involved a woman named Belva Lockwood, the second a woman named Lavinia Goodell. Lockwood had been in touch with Myra Bradwell since the early days of the *Chicago Legal News*, when she was accumulating rejections from law schools in the Washington, D.C., area. Lockwood could not leave the nation's capital because her husband was a minister there. In the pages of the *Chicago Legal News*, Bradwell had publicized Lockwood's struggle, culminating with a letter from the president of Columbian College, in Washington, D.C., informing Lockwood that "such admission would not be expedient as it would be likely to distract the attention of the young men."[14]

In 1870, Lockwood and fourteen other women were admitted to the newly formed National University Law School when the school found itself short on enrollments. The male student body treated the woman students so badly that only Lockwood and Lydia Hall stuck it out past the first semester.

One reason male students were so antagonistic was that degrees from universities that excluded women were considered far more prestigious than those earned at coed schools. Right before graduation day, a group of male students threatened to boycott the ceremonies if Lockwood and Hall were present. Not only did the administration ban the two women from the graduation exercises and delete their names from the program, but it withheld their hard-earned diplomas as well.

Hall, tired of the notoriety, dropped the fight, but Lockwood refused to give up. Denied admission to Washington, D.C.'s court because she had no law degree, Lockwood had managed to practice in a few lower courts while completing her law studies.

In 1873, Lockwood wrote to the president of the United States, Ulysses S. Grant, who also happened to be National University Law School's president, forcefully demanding her diploma. Two weeks later it came in the mail with no accompanying letter. A decade later National University Law School remained male only.

After two bar exams and a few court actions, Lockwood was finally admitted to the district bar in Washington, D.C. But the Lockwood case was far from over. Her cause became a vehicle for Bradwell to take on the federal courts and finally the U.S. Supreme Court itself.

Lockwood specialized in suits against the government. When she filed a client's appeal to the Federal Court of Claims, the court refused to admit her. It was one of the many disabilities for women lawyers. Even if they jumped the hurdles to practice law in their own states, they were not permitted to appeal to federal courts or the Supreme Court since they were not admitted to practice before these courts. The *Chicago Legal News* covered the events blow by blow. Nothing had changed. Chief Judge Charles Drake of the United States Court of Claims heard Lockwood's plea for admission, peered down at her, and said, "Mistress Lockwood, you are a woman,"[15] and refused to allow her to speak in her own behalf.

No one was surprised at Judge Drake's decision that woman was without legal capacity to take the office of attorney. Lockwood prepared the legal documents for her client and had him read them in court himself, since any citizen is permitted to plead his or her own case.

In the fall of 1876, Lockwood decided to jump over the lower federal courts and apply for permission to litigate before the United States Supreme Court. Her acceptance would mean that she could then practice in any federal court—or so she thought. In its written requirements for admission the Supreme Court made no mention of women but referred to "any attorney in good standing."

This time the decision came in a week. Chief Justice Morrison R. Waite once again relied on English common law, writing: ". . . none but men are admitted to practice before it as attorneys and counselors. This is in accordance with immemorial usage in England."

With her usual tart precision and sense of humor, Bradwell wrote:

Counselors have never been allowed to practice in Westminster Hall, and other superior courts in England unless they wore gowns and wigs, and therefore it follows that they should not be allowed to practice in the Supreme Court of the United States without these necessary articles.[16]

Bradwell and Lockwood next drafted a bill giving women lawyers access to federal courts. They convinced a friendly congressman to at least present it to the House Judiciary Committee. They waited for two years, and in 1878, "An Act to Relieve Certain Legal Disabilities of Women," passed the House of Representatives and moved on to the Senate. After a massive almost single-handed campaign by Bradwell and Lockwood, the legislation passed and was signed into law by President Rutherford Hayes in February 1879. A month later Lockwood was admitted to the Court of Claims and shortly thereafter became the first woman lawyer to argue a case before the U.S. Supreme Court, winning a $5 million settlement for the Cherokee Indian Nation to compensate for the theft of their lands.

But even in the face of her admission to practice before the Supreme Court, there were judges in the state courts steadfastly refusing to allow women lawyers into their courtrooms.[17] When Lockwood tried to file a lawsuit for a client in Maryland in 1878, she was turned away by a judge who said, "I pray to God that the time may never come when the State of Maryland will admit women to the Bar."[18]

While the decision in the Lockwood case was still pending, Bradwell went to the aid of another struggling woman lawyer, Lavinia Goodell, in Wisconsin. Like Lockwood, Goodell had been admitted to a circuit court but could not represent her clients in higher-court appeals.

Justice Edward Ryan of the Wisconsin Supreme Court, well known as an unshakable opponent of women's suffrage, did not even attempt to stick with legal arguments. First he complimented Goodell, "whose character raises no personal objection—something, perhaps, not always to be looked for in women who forsake the ways of their sex for the ways of ours,"and acknowledged that other courts had indeed admitted women. He then went on to sing Justice Bradley's old song, with somewhat stronger lyrics.

The law of nature . . . qualified the female sex for the bearing and nurture of the children of our race, and for the custody of the homes of the world. . . .

Since Goodell was unmarried and presumably not about to "bear and nurture" children, he discussed single women as well. The "cruel chances of life . . . may leave women free from the peculiar duties of their sex," he wrote. These women may need to work, he admitted, but the profession of law was not an appropriate one. Women were too delicate "to mix professionally in all the nastiness of the world which finds its way into the courts of justice; all the unclean issues . . . sodomy, incest, rape, seduction, fornication, adultery, pregnancy." He then publicly vowed, "If, as counsel threatened, these things are to come, we will take no voluntary part in bringing them about."[19]

Although it took several years, the Wisconsin legislature eventually passed a law modeled on Bradwell and Hulett's Illinois legislation that barred sex discrimination. But Judge Ryan still refused to admit Goodell. So Bradwell launched an impeachment campaign against him in the pages of the *Chicago Legal News*. In March 1877, the Wisconsin legislature revised a recently passed equal employment statute to make it read even more specifically: "No person shall be denied admission or license to practice *as an attorney in any court of this state* on account of sex." (Italics added.) Almost two years later, another judge finally granted Goodell her license, with Judge Ryan still protesting.

At last Goodell was able to concentrate on her practice. She did so well that she was able to take in a partner, Angie King, a student at the University of Chicago. Goodell and King won several difficult cases. In 1880, only a year after her victory, Goodell died at the age of forty-one. *The Chicago Journal* published news of her death and asked whether women are able to endure the hard usage and severe mental application incidental to a legal professional career.

Bradwell fumed. This was not the first time a friend had died and newspapers had used the sad event to propagandize against women attorneys. In 1874, Bradwell's friend Alta Hulett had passed away at the age of twenty-three. Again some newspapers considered this "proof" that women should stay away from the legal profession. At that time Bradwell had retaliated by discussing the early deaths of "a number of male members of the profession . . . recently stricken by the relentless hand of death, who were young, strong and vigorous."[20]

This time, Bradwell was less tactful, raising the possibility that Judge Ryan's long-term badgering of Goodell could very well have helped ruin her health. When Judge Ryan died, Myra Bradwell's obituary in the *Chicago Legal News* made no attempt to conceal her anger. She did not hesitate to mention his "ungovernable temper."

Stories of women's lack of stamina in the courtroom persisted for decades. In 1881, Anne C. Southworth, a Massachusetts law student, wrote an essay in which she commented on the hypocrisy involved in this "concern."

> Men for years have watched woman grow thin and stoop shouldered as she passes in the gray of early dawn and the shadow of the evening to and from the great factories. They have seen the hectic flush rising in her pale cheeks and have heard the hollow cough; perhaps they have even shaken their heads and solemnly predicted that such close confinement was killing or at least enervating her; but they have never seriously objected to allowing her to kill herself in that manner if she chose.[21]

47

In 1875, Bradwell spent a great deal of time on yet another matter, a mission of supreme delicacy and controversy: the fact that a woman's husband could declare her insane and send her off to a mental institution without even a court hearing. Apparently, a son, with just a few more requirements, could do the same.

When no one else would act, Bradwell, using any means necessary, rushed to rescue Abraham Lincoln's widow, Mary Todd Lincoln, from the clutches of her only surviving son, Robert Todd Lincoln. The Bradwells and Lincolns had been friends in the pre–Civil War days before Lincoln was elected president. After Lincoln's assassination, Mrs. Lincoln's life had become terribly bleak and she became an ardent, even compulsive, shopper. The money she spent came from the interest earned from her own estate, valued at more than $100,000. Perhaps her son worried that she would begin depleting the principal as well and he would inherit less, or perhaps he was embarrassed over the gossip. Whatever his motivation, he carried out actions that brought Myra Bradwell into head-on conflict with him.

When Mrs. Lincoln visited her son on March 12, 1875, he hired a detective to follow her around for three weeks. Then he asked six physicians to write reports on his mother's sanity. Four of them never even met Mrs. Lincoln, and the other two never professionally interviewed her. Nevertheless they all agreed that she was insane, and Robert Lincoln filed for an insanity hearing on May 19. Mrs. Lincoln was informed of the event one hour before the kangaroo court took place. Robert Lincoln's attorney provided a counsel for her on the spot.

Seventeen "witnesses" came forward with receipts proving that Mrs. Lincoln had "shopped till she dropped," a practice not then the widespread hobby it is today. Robert Lincoln also testified about his mother's spending habits. No witnesses appeared on Mrs. Lincoln's behalf. Neither the Bradwells nor any of Mrs. Lincoln's other friends even knew that the trial was taking place! After a few minutes, an all-male jury unanimously declared her insane.

Mrs. Lincoln was shipped off to a mental hospital for wealthy women in Batavia, Illinois. Not even permitted to write or receive letters, Mrs. Lincoln managed to smuggle a few notes out of the hospital. One was addressed to the Bradwells.[22] Myra Bradwell dropped everything and rushed to Batavia.

Refused the right to see Mrs. Lincoln, Bradwell launched a publicity campaign. When the headline appeared asking, "Is the Widow of President Lincoln a Prisoner?", followed by a story of Bradwell's not being given permission to visit her friend, the embarrassed head of the institution finally admitted Bradwell. Determining that her friend was in no way insane, Bradwell, knowing that a court appeal would achieve nothing, took a few extralegal steps to secure Mrs. Lincoln's freedom.

First she obtained the agreement of Mrs. Lincoln's sister to take her in after her release was accomplished. Then she sneaked the editor of the *Chicago Times*, Frank B. Wilkie, into Mrs. Lincoln's room so that he could judge her mental state.

Robert Todd Lincoln fumed when he learned that Bradwell had visited his mother, and he ordered Dr. Patterson, the head of the hospital, to deny the Bradwells future access to his mother because it would "tend to unsettle her mind." This only made the Bradwells more suspicious. On August 24, when Mrs. Lincoln had already spent almost four months incarcerated by her son, Wilkie published a story of his visit with "a perfectly sound and healthy" Mrs. Lincoln and also his interview with "an extremely reluctant Myra Bradwell."

Other newspapers picked up the story, calling for Mrs. Lincoln's immediate release. In less than two weeks, Robert Todd Lincoln took his mother to her sister's house in Springfield. Within the year she was officially declared sane by the Cook County Court and once again had control over her own trust fund.

Myra Bradwell had defeated Robert Todd Lincoln, by any means necessary, fair or foul. Mary Todd Lincoln showered the Bradwells with gifts and credited them with saving her.[23] She also sent a bitter letter to her son, telling him, "you have tried your game of robbery long enough."

With Mrs. Lincoln rescued, Bradwell returned to concentrate on the issue of the admission of women to law schools. As industrialization spread and the federal government expanded, educated professionals were much in demand. Colleges and law schools opened throughout the nation. A college degree followed by a law school degree became the norm for attorneys in the job market. Soon it became obvious that to land a spot in a prestigious law firm or the government, a degree from Harvard, Yale, or Columbia, the most prestigious Ivy League schools, was worth far more than graduation from other law schools. Women were barred from the elite schools, and although it seemed futile to try, a few women attempted to break down the barriers. Lemma Barkaloo, born in Brooklyn, New York, was one such woman. Barkaloo had been the first to apply for admission to Columbia University in 1868, along with two other young women, giving Columbia the dubious distinction of being the first Ivy League law school to reject women. Columbia's George Templeton Strong entered in his diary:

> Application from three infatuated young women to the Law School. No woman shall degrade herself by practicing law in New York especially if I can save her. . . . "Women's Rights Women" are uncommonly loud and offensive of late. I loathe the lot.[24]

50

Mary Todd Lincoln, widow of President Abraham Lincoln, was committed to an insane asylum by her son.

Strong was not only adamant about keeping women away from Columbia but also Jewish applicants. In 1874 he pushed for "either a college diploma or an examination including Latin" for entrance to the Law School. "This will keep out the little scrubs (*German Jew boys mostly*)."[25] (Original italics.)

The reasons given for excluding women were often patently ridiculous. In the 1870s two women, Ellen Martin and M. Frederika Perry, applied to Harvard Law School and were told that the school could not "admit young men and young women to the law library at the same time, and it is not considered fair to admit them to the Law School without giving them privileges to the Library."[26]

In 1872, a prominent Yale alumnus wrote a letter of "recommendation" to Yale's administrators for the admission of a woman acquaintance. It can be presumed that the woman never saw the letter. "Are you far advanced enough to admit young women to your school?" he asked. "In theory I am in favor of their studying and practicing law, provided they are ugly, but I should fear a handsome woman before a jury."[27] In the face of such obstacles, no other woman again attempted to knock at the hallowed doors of the Halls of Ivy until 1885.

It was difficult in all parts of the nation for women to enter the law profession, but in the burgeoning cities of the East, it was just about impossible. The idea of the "woman's sphere" was easier to enforce there than in the labor-short West, where many women worked alongside men. Several eastern-born women, including Lemma Barkaloo and Lavinia Goodell, relocated and received their education elsewhere rather than face a losing battle.

In 1870, Carrie Burnham Kilgore, the first woman in New York State to win a degree in medicine in 1864, tried for another first when she applied to the University of Pennsylvania Law School. Rejected, she attempted to buy individual tickets to attend lectures. One of the law professors, E. Spencer Miller, ungrammatically told her: "I do not know what the Board of Trustees will do, but as for me, if they admit a woman I will resign for I will neither lecture to niggers nor women."[28]

Eleven years later, Kilgore tried again, this time sending her husband to purchase the lecture passes. The Board of Trustees quickly informed her that even if she attended every required lecture and passed all of the examinations, they would not guarantee that she would earn a diploma. Later Kilgore said, "It is impossible to appreciate the intense opposition to my admission to the University. . . . Now people . . . wonder if there really was opposition. The necessity for police protection was quite seriously discussed at the University."[29]

Initially refused admission to the Pennsylvania bar, Kilgore managed in 1883 to win admission to a lower court. Three years later she was admitted to litigate before the Pennsylvania Supreme Court. She was the only woman lawyer in the "City of Brotherly Love" for at least ten years.

In the 1870s, Boston University admitted women, but the state of Massachusetts banned women from bar admission. Lelia J. Robinson, a Boston University honors graduate in 1879, spent over a year fighting for bar admission. She never forgot that year. Over the next decade she researched the issue of discrimination against women law students and lawyers, publishing her depressing findings in a legal magazine.

It remained a little easier for women in the Midwest to enter law schools. An occasional one, like the State University of Iowa, admitted several women. The Iowa administration also made sure, by sending people to accompany them to their classes, that women would not be tormented in classes. Mary B. Hickey was the first woman to graduate from Iowa State in 1873, and each decade the enrollments increased. The law school of the University of Michigan at Ann Arbor also admitted some women.

Lemma Barkaloo, after her Columbia University rejection as well as dozens of others, went on to become the first woman law student in the United States as well as Missouri's first woman lawyer. Amazingly, the Law Department of Washington University in St. Louis, Missouri, accepted her. She attended her first classes in the fall of 1869. One professor claimed that Barkaloo "seemed to enjoy the embarrassment of the young men very much," but since she quit after her first year of school, it is dubious that her pleasure amounted to much. She passed the Missouri bar exam but died soon after during a typhoid epidemic in 1870. Eight years later the *United States Biographical Dictionary* said that Lemma Barkaloo had "died of over-mental exertion."[30]

Phoebe Couzins, Barkaloo's classmate, stayed on to graduate. When she did, she thanked the university officials for their fair treatment of "one whose soul has been sadly torn and bruised by endless friction with the carping spirits and narrow minds of today."[31] Couzins was admitted to the bar in Missouri, Kansas, and Utah, and later to federal courts. She briefly served as a U.S. Marshall, completing her father's term when he died suddenly.

But the few Midwestern state universities open to women were exceptions to the rule of not permitting women to study law. Moreover, the majority of law schools and men in the legal profession continued their often demeaning behavior toward women lawyers. Newspaper reporters were especially upset by even the possibility of prestigious appointments for women attorneys. In 1882, for example, when someone suggested that President Chester Arthur appoint Phoebe Couzins to the commission regulating the Utah territory, a *St. Louis Spectator* editorial declared that women "are totally unfit to enter into the courts and practice law."[32] Couzins did not get the job.

Every step of the way was a fresh struggle. In 1878, the University of California announced the establishment of the Hastings College of Law, made possible through an endowment from Judge Clinton Hastings. Women would not be welcomed, Judge Hastings declared, because they would "distract the male students by their rustling garments."[33]

Once again a woman of valor, Clara Shortridge Foltz, California's first woman attorney, challenged the Hastings administration. Once again, one single staunch ally, Myra Bradwell, was there to help her.[34] Perhaps Judge Hastings underestimated his adversary. Clara Foltz, the first woman attorney in California, had fought for her career every step of the way.

She had arrived in California in 1874. At the age of twenty-five, she already had five children. Two years later she divorced her husband and decided to study for the bar in the office of a sympathetic lawyer. Anticipating that the California Supreme Court would refuse to admit her no matter how high her bar examination score, Foltz determined to change the California law. She found an ally in Laura De Force Gordon, who was well-known for her unfaltering struggle for women's rights and her tough demands on women. Gordon had once told a group of women at a suffrage meeting "not to sit like mummies but to open their mouths and vote audibly. This disinclination to do business in a business-like way is discreditable."[35]

Together Foltz and Gordon fought for legislation to change the words in the state code on bar admission from "any white male citizen" to "any citizen or person." After months of hard work by the women, Senate Bill 66, known as the Woman Lawyer's Bill, was approved by both houses of the state legislature.

Foltz sailed through the bar exam and was admitted to the 20th District Court Bar in the fall of 1878. In a few months she had a growing practice in San Jose. [36]

Neither Foltz nor Gordon was willing to drop the battle for the admission of women to the Hastings College of Law. In one of the earliest sit-ins in American history, Foltz and Gordon walked into the school, were refused registration, and occupied seats in the required classes. Many male students quickly engaged in a mocking game of "monkey see, monkey do," imitating every cough and movement of the two women. The college board immediately ordered the two women tossed out. Gordon and Foltz rushed off to file suit against Hastings in California Supreme Court.

Their claim was legally sound. Since Hastings was part of the University of California, and the university admitted women, there was no legal basis on which to bar them. Hastings' lawyers attempted to prove that since Hastings had received private funding, it was not part of the University of California. After a court victory, Foltz officially attended her first classes on January 9, 1879, but the fight was far from over.

First a letter from Judge Hastings informed her that her admission still required approval by the board of directors. In her classes, the students continued their games, assuming that the college authorities would find a way to get rid of her if her presence disrupted class proceedings. "You would have thought the whooping cough was a raging epidemic among the little fellows," Foltz later said, describing her reception.

After two days of this nonsense she received the expected notification that her application for admission had been denied. Back to court she trudged with Gordon by her side. Hastings's attorney cited cases where judges had used the "law of nature" to ban women from law practice. He referred to Foltz's "beauty" and said that a jury would not be able to judge fairly when she pleaded a case. Yet press reports on the case added not so subtle hints that the two women were less than "feminine." They printed details of Gordon's "stylish black dress with some suggestions of masculinity in the make" and Foltz's hands "not lacking in bone and muscle."[37]

Foltz remained calm, telling the judge that she had expected legal arguments, and that she more than met all of the entrance requirements. Apparently, the judge agreed, ruling in favor of the women. No doubt in an effort to wear down Foltz and Gordon emotionally and financially, the Hastings board of directors appealed. While the case pended, the women attended classes. Foltz was admitted to the State Supreme Court bar in December 1879 and successfully represented herself against the Hastings lawyers during their appeal. Later she described that case as "the greatest in my more than half century before the bar."

Foltz went on to be appointed the first woman Los Angeles deputy district attorney. She also created California's parole system and public defender system. The work she did probably made a huge difference to literally thousands of poor men and women. Despite these remarkable achievements, Foltz continued to find herself the object of ridicule in courtrooms. At one trial the prosecutor publicly stated that it would be better if Foltz had stayed home to care for her children. Foltz's rapid response was: "A woman had better be in almost any business than raising such men as you."

In another case, the prosecutor, in his closing remarks to the jury, warned them: "She is a woman; she cannot be expected to reason . . . this young woman will lead you by her sympathetic presentation of this case to violate your oaths and let a guilty man go free."[38] Foltz had already made her closing remarks but she was granted permission to address the court and won her case.

In 1879, after a ten-year running battle, Myra Bradwell was able to announce that twenty-six women had been admitted to the bar in seven states. But in thirty states, "the laws are such that a woman would be refused admission by the bar, simply on account of her sex."[39]

Despite the hard-won victories, most of the pioneer women lawyers knew that on this state-by-state, one-by-one basis, it would take decades for women to gain an effective presence in the legal profession. It was clear that only federal legislation would bring a noticeable change, and as long as women could not vote, the power to make laws remained in the hands of men. Suffrage, many of them believed, was the key, and several woman lawyers worked to achieve that goal.

As usual, ridicule was the favorite weapon used against women's suffrage advocates. A Boston newspaper praised a man who "with a wedding kiss shuts up the mouth of Lucy Stone." Her husband, Henry Blackwell, supported Stone totally. They edited the word *obey* out of their wedding ceremony, and Lucy kept her own name.

Just as the issue of the black vote had broken the early women's rights movement in two, so too racism continued to haunt the suffrage movement. The state-by-state method had very few successes, and Susan B. Anthony and her supporters wanted an all-out push for a constitutional amendment. But the Southern Woman Suffrage Conference held firmly to the "states' rights" position, as did the former slaveholders. The southern women believed they could win the vote from southern legislatures only if they could guarantee that black men would lose their voting rights and black women never get theirs.[40]

For African Americans in the South and Hispanics in the Southwest, at the mercy of their state governments, not only voting rights but just about all of their civil rights were in jeopardy. In 1876, federal troops were withdrawn from the South and Reconstruction was to all intents and purposes dead. Segregationist laws called "black codes" were passed throughout the South, and the Ku Klux Klan enforced them with whips and lynching ropes. By 1895 most black men had been excluded from voting. Black women, of course, had never been allowed to vote. There wasn't even a hint of revival of the old coalition between those who supported black civil rights and women's rights advocates. As allies the groups might have changed history. Instead, women and all minorities—blacks, Latinos, Asians, and Native Americans—found themselves largely shut out of the "American Dream."

3

TWO STRIKES: GENDER; THREE STRIKES: RACE

Man has been trying to do the housekeeping in
the Temple of Justice for years all by himself,
with the result of cobwebs all over the place. . . .
It needs women's wit, women's fairness and
women's sense of right and righteousness to put
the legal fabric in order and repair

—*Phoebe Couzins at the founding*
meeting of the Alumnae Association of the
Women's Legal Education Society in 1895[1]

On the brink of the twentieth century, the situation for women aspiring to be lawyers remained discouraging. In 1880, after a decade of one-by-one victories, there were only about 200 women lawyers. By 1910, with the population exploding, there were only 559, less than 1 percent of the vastly expanded legal profession.[2]

In medicine, women did somewhat better, despite new obstacles placed in their way. Fresh scientific discoveries had revolutionized medicine in Europe in the 1880s. Americans who studied abroad returned home and pressed for the "professionalization" of medicine. In the East, a group of wealthy women offered half a million dollars to Harvard if they would accept women into their medical school. Harvard turned them down, but Johns Hopkins University in Baltimore, Maryland, accepted the conditions and built a new medical school in 1893. As other schools dropped their own barriers, women soon composed one quarter to one third of the nation's medical school students.

Because of the increase in coed medical education, all except three of the seventeen women's medical schools closed their doors. It appeared at first that women's decisions to enter coed institutions had been wise. During this so-called "Gilded Age," the number of women doctors rose from a 2,423 in 1880 to more than 7,000 by 1900.[3]

As the federal government expanded in the decades following the Civil War, Washington, D.C., drew thousands of people into government jobs, among them a sprinkling of women. African American men composed more than 10 percent of nearly 25,000 federal employees, although most of them held the lowest-paying clerical positions. The number of white male lawyers skyrocketed. They seemed to be everywhere, representing businesses and banks, in private practice, elected as congressmen and senators, in the federal courtrooms. Even a few African American male lawyers were seen, although in the entire nation there were less than 700 black members of bar, most of them graduates of Howard University.

But the "Gilded Age" left would-be women lawyers out in the cold. White women lawyers remained a rare sight, while African American and Hispanic women lawyers were simply never seen. The rift between abolitionists and suffragists after the Civil War, as well as the new post-Reconstruction racist atmosphere, helped to erect a towering wall of invisibility around black and Latina women.

Even the administrators at Howard and other black colleges, who had taken a leaf from Frederick Douglass's book and supported women's rights, made an exception when it came to admissions to law school! Howard Medical School, on the other hand, from the day its doors opened, admitted all qualified students—black, white, male, female.[4]

Mexican American women, many of whose ancestors had settled the Southwest and California long before the *Mayflower* arrived, could not even dream of careers. In 1848, as the women in Seneca Falls met to discuss women's rights, the U.S.–Mexico War was ending. Before and after that war, Mexican Americans lost their land and their rights, either through the violent attacks of newly arriving white settlers or the chicanery and corruption of the courts. Many Mexican Americans went to work as agricultural laborers on ranches they once had owned. Latinos throughout the nation became what has been called "the invisible minority," an unfortunate status imposed on them until the 1970s.[5]

For African Americans, lack of educational opportunities remained a major barrier. In most southern states before the Civil War, it was illegal to even teach the alphabet to slaves. Only a few managed secretly to learn to read and write. Slavery, after all, had been "justified" by a solid "scientific" rationale of black inferiority. An educated slave not only disproved the theories of mental deficiency but also made black men and women more likely to read "dangerous material" and run away or organize struggles for freedom.

In the non-slave states, too, black children were banned from attending schools, even those supported by taxes collected from their parents. Private schools were also carefully watched in case their directors developed "funny" ideas about integration.

The most famous such administrator was a white Quaker woman, Prudence Crandall, who ran a school for young ladies in Canterbury, Connecticut. In 1833, when Crandall enrolled one young black girl, Sarah Harris, in her school, the parents of the other students quickly removed their children from classes and organized a boycott. Local physicians and shopkeepers refused the school their services.

When Crandall stood her ground and bravely held classes for seventeen black children, the Connecticut legislature passed a law prohibiting Connecticut citizens from teaching any "person of color" not living in the state. Crandall was jailed for "harboring vagrants."

Crandall continued to defy the law and was arrested and tried three times. At her third trial she was convicted when the judge instructed the jury that blacks were not to be viewed as citizens even if they lived in a free state. The conviction was later reversed on a technicality, and Crandall struggled to keep her school open until a firebombing forced her to close it down.

Despite the obvious hardships and dangers, other brave women followed in Crandall's footsteps. In 1850, Myrtilla Miner made plans to open a teachers' training school for black women in Washington, D.C. Miner realized that before black children could be widely educated, black teachers would have to be prepared to do the job. Frederick Douglass tried to talk her out of it, fearful of seeing "this little woman harassed by the law, insulted in the street, the victim of slave-holding malice, and possibly, beaten down by the mob."[6]

But despite Douglass's fears, Miner went out fundraising. Harriet Beecher Stowe, the best-selling author of the most famous antislavery novel, *Uncle Tom's Cabin*, donated the then huge sum of $1,000. In the fall of 1851, Miner Teachers College enrolled six young students and soon expanded to forty. Like Crandall's school, Miner's school was constantly under attack. In 1860, as the movement to end slavery grew stronger, an arsonist set fire to the building, destroying much of it. The school continued for a short time, but Miner's health had deteriorated. She died in 1864 at the age of forty-nine.

Among Miner's last graduates was a young girl who would go on to become the first African American woman lawyer in the United States, Charlotte E. Ray. Prior to her accomplishment, two black women were known to have appeared before courts in their own behalf. Mumbet, a slave woman who used the name Elizabeth Freeman, took her demand for freedom to a Massachusetts court in 1783. Under the Massachusetts Bill of Rights, she won her claim that as a native-born American, she was a free woman. The first woman to argue a case before the United States Supreme Court was also an African American, Lucy Terry Prince (1730–1821). When a white colonel attempted to take the Prince family farm in Vermont, they went to court, lost their case, and appealed. When the case reached the Supreme Court, Lucy Prince decided to argue it herself in 1796—and won! Chief Justice Samuel Chase said that Prince had made a better argument than he had heard from any lawyer at the Vermont bar.[7]

Charlotte Ray was born in New York City on January 13, 1850, one of seven children in a free black family.[8] Her minister father, Charles Bennett Ray, was a conductor on the "Underground Railroad." Her parents, like those of so many pioneer women lawyers, ardently believed in the education of daughters as well as sons.

Immediately after the Civil War, chances to receive an education improved for African Americans when the federal government's Reconstruction programs made schools and hospitals a priority. Volunteer black and white teachers headed south to work in the Freedman's Bureau educational campaign, trying to make a dent in the 95 percent illiteracy rate. More than a quarter of a million children attended over 4,000 schools during the all too brief era of Reconstruction.[9]

Several black colleges were also opened, including Fisk University, Hampton Institute, and Howard University. When it came to higher education, black men by far were the major recipients of the short-lived benefits. By 1890 only thirty black women held college degrees.

Charlotte Ray was hired as a teacher in the teacher's training department at Howard in 1869, but her real ambition was to study law. She applied to Howard Law School as "C. E. Ray" (to disguise her sex) and managed to slip through the gender barriers. Once having admitted her, Howard was too embarrassed to expel one of its own teachers. A year later, the annual report of the law school mentioned that C. E. Ray, "a colored woman . . . read us a thesis on corporations, not copied from books but from her brain, a clear incisive analysis."[10]

Several of the black men in Ray's class of 1869–1872 went on to establish successful practices, many in the Washington, D.C., area. Charlotte Ray did not do as well, even though she was among the top students in her graduating class. With a specialty in corporate law, she passed the bar examination in the District of Columbia and was admitted to practice on April 23, 1872. But she was unable to attract enough clients from the business world to earn a living. After five years of struggle, in 1879 she gave up and went back to New York City, where she taught in a Brooklyn public school. Ray died in 1911, nine years before women were allowed to vote.

In the 1880s three other black women graduated from Howard Law School. Only one of them, Mary Ann Shadd Cary—a sixty-one-year-old principal in one of Washington, D.C.'s segregated schools and a leader in the abolitionist movement—earned a modest living practicing law until her death in 1893. Elsewhere, the picture was the same for African Americans. Ida B. Platt graduated from Chicago Law School in 1892, a year before Myra Bradwell's death, but was barred from practice by the Illinois bar. Lutie Lytle, was admitted to the Tennessee bar, but little is known about her activities.

Just as the doors to Howard Law School were opening a crack for women, Reconstruction ended and the long dark night of black codes and Jim Crow began. With government financing withdrawn, the all-black colleges had to limp along as best as they could without federal support.

As the virus of racism spread to every section of the nation, the slim gains of African Americans deteriorated quickly. By the 1920s, instead of the paltry 115 black women doctors that practiced at the turn of the century, there were only about sixty-five! In the legal profession, not another word was heard about a black woman lawyer for decades.

The two factions of the women's movement that had split over the question of black male suffrage right after the Civil War reunited in 1890. But two years later the "moderates" of NAWSA passed a resolution that made it clear that the organization would fight for the voting rights of white women in open preference to suffrage for black and immigrant women and men. When the Supreme Court reversed the Civil Rights Act of 1875 and three years later handed down the "separate but equal" decision in *Plessy* v. *Ferguson* (1896), there wasn't even a whisper of protest from the suffrage movement.

Blacks were legally free, but their economic conditions had changed very little. Most black women were stuck in agricultural or domestic work. African American women, like women everywhere, were told that young men deserved schooling first. As one scholar phrased it, "Many a male Negro received education or a start in a small business through the laborious efforts of the woman in the household over the washtub or ironing board."[11]

Anna J. Cooper, a turn-of-the-century African American teacher in Washington, D.C., had plenty to say about black men's lack of interest in the education of black women.

> While our men seem thoroughly abreast of the times on every other subject, when they strike the woman question they drop back into 16th-century logic.[12]

Phoebe Couzins, Utah's first woman lawyer, was one of the few white women who spoke out forcefully on the rights of *all* women: "Black women are, and always have been, in far worse condition than the men," she said.[13] But most of the pioneer women lawyers, activists in numerous reform movements, especially suffrage, shied away from the controversial issues of race.

Myra Bradwell's *Chicago Legal News* made scant mention of the problems of aspiring black women lawyers. Then, in 1884, when Ada Kepley was denied admission to the bar in Chicago at around the same time that a black man was admitted, Bradwell wrote "The woman in the race to obtain the legal right to practice law in Illinois has been outdistanced by the Negro."

Bradwell's biographer speculated that "Perhaps Myra's intention . . . was not to appeal to racial sentiments, but merely to demonstrate that her own sex was, in some respects, enslaved to a far greater degree than was the Negro race."[14] But that doesn't explain Bradwell's lack of interest in black women, who lived under the double oppression of racism and sexism. Bradwell, who kept close tabs on women law students and graduates throughout the nation, must have known that white women, when they were unable to pursue law studies elsewhere, often were admitted to Howard University.

For a long time black women understandably gave up on entering the legal profession. If a woman like Charlotte Ray could not earn a living despite her obvious talents, it seemed impossible for any black women to succeed. Furthermore, the economic and psychological survival of millions of African Americans must have seemed a far more important "cause" than entry into the professions. Most employers as well as the early labor unions barred African Americans from jobs and membership. Not only schools but many hospitals turned them away—even the children. Ku Klux Klan members were never punished for beating and lynching black people.

With the days of the abolitionist movement long past, allies were few and far between. Many better-off white women spent much of their time in women's clubs, dedicated to a wide variety of social reforms. By 1890 the club movement had grown so large that a General Federation of Women's Clubs was formed to coordinate their work.

Although a few black women continued to press for suffrage, most African American activists concentrated on the far more urgent concerns. The crusade for antilynching legislation, led by Ida B. Wells, a black woman born to slave parents only a few months before the Emancipation Proclamation, must have seemed a far more worthwhile cause than suffrage or efforts to break into the professions.

Ida B. Wells's antilynching work led to the formation of black women's organizations in 1892. They appealed for cooperation between the black and white women's groups, but made no headway. In 1900 at the convention of the General Federation of Women's Clubs, the credentials committee excluded the black delegate sent by a leading African American women's club.[15]

Many of the pioneer women lawyers had been motivated to study law in order to change the lives of less fortunate women. On a Saturday afternoon in February 1887, a group of women lawyers gathered for their regular Equity Club meeting. Their subject was: "What

Is Our Duty As Women Lawyers in Society?" Most of them agreed with the opening statement: "I believe that as Women Lawyers . . . we must make a special effort, also, outside of our profession, for other women besides ourselves."[16]

Clara Foltz, California's first woman lawyer, was a shining example of that philosophy. She spent her entire professional life fighting for equal justice for all.[17] Poor people accused of crimes were assigned *unpaid* court-appointed attorneys who were supposed to devise ways to collect their fees from their often penniless clients. The only lawyers willing to work for the usual zero fee were recent graduates who needed practice in court-room procedures, older lawyers who had bad reputations, and, of course, women lawyers. There was no money available for private investigators, expert testimony, or any of the other advantages enjoyed by more prosperous defendants. Without these "frills," conviction by an experienced and often well-paid public prosecutor was almost a certainty.

Foltz drafted legislation creating a government-funded public defender system providing legal representation to poor defendants. Her bill was not enacted in California until 1921 and did not become national law until the mid-1960s! Foltz also was instrumental in the creation of California's prison parole system as well as laws separating juvenile offenders from adult prisoners.

Like other women lawyers, Foltz was a frequent target of press ridicule. But she told friends that most painful of all were the "wounds which women inflicted upon me . . . who even refused friendly recognition of my efforts."[18]

Nevertheless, several of the pioneer women lawyers chose to buck the prejudices against women in criminal law courts and urged others to do the same. Martha Strickland, admitted to the Michigan bar in 1883, spoke out against the exclusion of women from juries. The U.S. Constitution entitled defendants to a jury of their peers, yet, Strickland said, ". . . women . . . are called upon every day to submit their dearest rights of happiness, property and life to the judgment of persons differently constituted, mentally and physically, from themselves . . . so . . . that the maxim . . . 'put yourself in his place' is impossible."[19]

As long as women could not register as voters, of course, they were not called for jury service. It also was almost impossible for them to "mount the bench." By 1900 only five women had been appointed or elected to even minor judicial roles. Two decades later there were only fifteen.

The suffrage movement's attempts to win the vote state by state bogged down quickly except in a few far-flung areas. In the territory of Wyoming in 1870, for example, a constitutional amendment granted women's suffrage. Amidst alarmist predictions of bloodshed, only a few women dared to vote, but newspapers reported that "rough mountaineers maintained the most respectful decorum whenever the women approached the polls."[20] Wyoming women began serving on juries as well. Myra Bradwell commented in the *Chicago Legal News*, "To all well educated, ambitious females, who have no legal ties to bind them, we would say, emigrate to Wyoming."[21]

That same year when the justice of the peace of South Pass City, J. H. Barr, resigned, Esther McQuigg Morris was appointed to his post. Morris, a milliner by trade, had played an important role in drafting and winning passage of Wyoming's Women's Suffrage Bill.

Barr quickly changed his mind and demanded a court hearing. Esther Morris's appointment was upheld, but that did not end the turmoil. Her husband, John Morris, a local saloonkeeper, came into court and created a noisy ruckus over his wife's new job. Esther Morris fined him and when he refused to pay, she packed him off to jail. Morris performed her job admirably for almost a year, and then stepped down, most probably because of the turmoil at home. Not one of the many cases she handled was reversed by a higher court.

In 1889, Wyoming applied for admission to the Union, maintaining its woman suffrage provision in its newly drafted state constitution. Susan B. Anthony listened from Congress's visitors' gallery while speakers argued that the Supreme Court *Minor* decision of 1874 prohibited women from voting in any state. The territorial delegate from Wyoming wired his legislature that they might have to drop their suffrage provision. "We will remain out of the Union a hundred years rather than come in without the women," the return message read.[22] After a close vote, Wyoming was admitted to the Union. Esther Morris, the first woman judge in the nation, presented the new flag to the governor.

A handful of other women also were named as justices in small towns. In 1884, Ada Lee, a graduate of the University of Michigan Law School, was elected on the joint ticket of the Republican, Democratic, and Greenback parties as circuit court commissioner. As thirteen suits to oust her pended, she tried over 200 cases and completed her term.

That same year, Marilla Young Ricker, the first woman lawyer in New Hampshire, was appointed U.S. commissioner. Aside from her regular duties, Ricker made weekly Sunday visits to prisoners and pushed hard for prison reform. Every year from 1870 on, Ricker demanded the right to vote before the selectmen of Dover, New Hampshire.

Hopes for a constitutional amendment granting women suffrage were not high. A friend of Susan B. Anthony had introduced the "Anthony Amendment" in 1878, a simple statement that "the right of citizens of the United States to vote shall not be denied or abridged by the United States or by any state on account of sex." Tabled year after year, the proposal reached the Senate floor in 1887. After days of long speeches by senators predicting the death of the American family, the amendment was defeated 34 to 16.

The suffrage movement lost steam as many of its activists realized that the state-by-state approach was not working. The same was true for women struggling to enter the legal profession. The Ivy League schools showed no sign of lessening their hostility toward the enrollment of women, and more and more the job market demanded "elite" diplomas. A handful of white women persisted in pounding on the locked doors of Yale, Columbia, and Harvard.

Alice Rufie Jordan showed up in the registrar's office at Yale in 1885, armed with a Bachelor of Science degree from the University of Michigan as well as her Michigan license to practice law. As she entered, the wild call of "fire," the typical greeting at all-male institutions whenever a woman came on the scene, swept over the area.

Told she could not register, Jordan stood her ground, pointing out that the Yale catalog said not one word about the exclusion of women. Jordan paid her fee and began attending classes. The university returned her tuition. Jordan kept the money and still showed up for courses taught by faculty members who agreed to grade her work.

Journalists came from other East Coast cities to cover the Jordan story. A reporter from the *New York Herald* was on hand when Jordan presented her assigned practice case during her second year at Yale. He had little to say on her performance but commented "she was attired in rich black silk that glittered with bead work."

Jordan actually earned a degree, but future Yale catalogues corrected the "error." In 1890, the first woman lawyer in Massachusetts, Lelia J. Robinson, requested and received Yale's catalog with a notation that "the marked paragraph on page 25 is intended to prevent a repetition of the Jordan incident."[23]

Most of the pioneer women lawyers apparently decided to stay away from losing battles and concentrate on carrying out the tasks set forth by the Equity Club lawyers. When a poor woman needed an attorney, she could almost always find a woman lawyer to help her out.

Despite the important role they played on behalf of the poor, women lawyers continued to be subjected to ridicule. The more socially concerned they were, the more the press railed against them. One woman in particular, Kansas lawyer Mary Clynen Lease, became a favorite target of newspapermen. They labeled her the "Wichita Cyclone," "Ironjawed Woman of Kansas," and the "Red Dragon." "Beware of her," journalists warned their female readers. "She advises you to defy the law of the land."

Lease's father, a Union soldier, had died in a Confederate prison during the Civil War. At the age of fifteen, Lease started working as a teacher to support her widowed mother and younger brothers and sisters. At eighteen she went to Kansas to take a higher paying job. In 1873 she married and soon was raising four children. All around her she saw farmers working terribly hard and yet growing poorer as railroad and storage companies made fortunes storing and shipping their wheat. Many of them lost their farms as banks foreclosed on their mortgages.

When the farmers organized to fight back, Mary Lease began to wish she had the legal training to help them. Lease studied law with a sympathetic local attorney and passed the Kansas bar examination in less than a year. She refused all fees, saying it is a "duty to help the poor and work for social justice."[24]

Lease often appeared as a speaker at rallies of the new farmers' Populist movement that spread through Kansas and ran many candidates in 1890. In one of her most quoted speeches, she told her cheering audience,

> The politicians said we suffered from overproduction. Yet 10,000 children starve to death every year in the United States. The common people are robbed to enrich their masters. . . . What you farmers need to do is to raise less corn and more hell![25]

Politicians seldom debated her points but instead snickered. When Senator John Ingalls of Kansas made the public comment that "Mrs. Lease had better be home mending her children's stockings," Lease campaigned against him throughout the state and had the satisfaction of seeing him go down in defeat. In 1900 Mary Clynen Lease moved to New York City, worked as a reporter for Joseph Pulitzer's *New York World*, and ran a free legal services office for poor immigrants.

Even the small gains made by women in the professions frightened enough men to produce a countermovement to squelch their feeble progress. In the late 1880s, a new field, called home management education, an obvious child of the Cult of Domesticity, was introduced at many coeducational colleges. Women were urged to major in this new home economics program—where they learned the latest "scientific" methods of housecleaning—rather than select the "male" fields of anthropology, chemistry, mathematics, medicine, and law.[26]

The women's rights movement had almost completely faded. There was no organization prepared to fight the new wave of efforts to "keep women in their place." As more wealthy women had joined the early professionals' quest for the vote, the struggling suffrage movement had become more conservative. A new generation of younger women took over the organizational reins of NAWSA and stayed away from controversial issues, hoping to keep the movement "respectable." They had no experience in the antislavery movement and little interest in other social issues.

During the 1880s and 1890s, as industrialization leaped forward and workers were needed, ships filled with European immigrants—Poles, Italians, Russians—arrived in New York harbor. Some, like the Russian Jews, were fleeing persecution. Labor recruiters for new industrialists had encouraged others to come, promising jobs and a new life. Many stayed where the boats docked, crowding into the tenements of the Lower East Side, East Harlem, and Brooklyn. Others moved on to Pittsburgh, Chicago, any cities where steel plants and meatpacking plants were springing up. There were jobs waiting in the mushrooming factories, but few schools and health services and little decent housing.

State referenda on women's suffrage failed seventeen times, winning in only two states, Colorado and Idaho. In 1896, Congress debated the Anthony Amendment and defeated it handily. It was not raised again until 1913.

In a few places, women were allowed to vote on school taxes and bond issues, and even occasionally in city elections. But as late as 1880, in New York State school board elections, men threw stones and spat at women voters. By 1891, nineteen states permitted women to vote in school elections and elect a few women to school boards.

Belva Lockwood joined with other California women and formed the Equal Rights Party in 1884. Lockwood ran for the U.S. presidency with Marietta L. Stow as her running mate. Despite a broad campaign mocking her in the press, supporters managed to get the party on the ballot in six states and she received over 4,000 all-

Belva Lockwood helped found the Equal Rights Party in 1884.

male votes. She repeated the effort four years later with Marilla Young Richer as her vice presidential candidate. But Lockwood and her supporters realized, of course, that women would never be elected to high office if they could not participate in elections.

Liquor interests were a major source of opposition to women's suffrage because many of the women who fought for voting rights also supported the Women's Christian Temperance Union, headed by Frances Willard. Willard was known for her notorious racist remarks about alcoholism among African Americans. Several pioneer women lawyers devoted much time and energy to the anti-alcohol crusade.[27] Women flooded into the WCTU in every state, eventually more than 200,000 of them. The liquor interests worried that if women voted, they would push through prohibition legislation. They spent a small fortune opposing women's suffrage state referenda.

A few of the middle-class and wealthy clubwomen devoted their spare time to a new cause—the education and "Americanization" of the new immigrants, especially the many young women. This early work would eventually burgeon into a flourishing settlement house movement in several cities. Mrs. Leonard Weber, the wife of a prominent doctor, at first believed that courses in cleaning and cooking were the most beneficial offerings for the new arrivals. But she soon discovered legal and economic problems plagued most immigrant women far more than lack of recipes.

Few of the immigrant women had the slightest knowledge of their legal rights in the United States, whether it was in cases of desertion and child support, or even things as simple as signing an agreement with a landlord. Mrs. Weber and Dr. Emily Kempin Spyri, a renowned law professor from Switzerland, opened a legal clinic, the Arbitration Society, where the women could come for assistance. They had many volunteers but few knew enough about the law to be of much help to the hundreds of women who flooded into their makeshift office. There were no women lawyers in the entire city of New York and only one in the whole state. Lemma Barkaloo, Lavinia Goodell, Belva Lockwood, all native New Yorkers, had left the state, finding it too difficult to further their careers there.

But Weber and Kempin were not about to give up. They appealed to administrators at the University of New York (later New York University—NYU). In 1890, the Women's Legal Education Society opened its doors in a building in Greenwich Village, offering adult education classes. For a yearly fee of five dollars, women could study the rudiments of law. At the end of each year, examinations were held and women were given certificates of completion at graduation ceremonies.

Reporters arrived to cover the first such ceremony, where several women made speeches on serious legal subjects. As usual, descriptions of the clothing and physical appearance of the women took the center stage in the next day's newspaper articles. One *New York Times* headline read "These Women Know Law but Don't Look At All Like Typical Lawyers." The story went on to describe the "pretty white dresses" and one speaker who "looked as charming as the proverbial sweet girl graduate." *The New York Continental* pronounced that "the valedictorian is pretty, piquant and lovable, rich in all the feminine graces and lives in the most artistic surroundings."[28] This type of coverage was the norm then, even as it is today. In 1893, the *Brooklyn Chronicle* profiled eight Brooklyn women who had completed the law course in exactly the same way. The headline read "Law Has Charms", and typical comments followed:

> A good deal of unusual cleverness is contained in her pretty little head with its wealth of dark braids. Mrs. Ruth Feriss Russell (wife of Profes-

sor Russell) is very pretty and exceedingly girlish, notwithstanding her legal knowledge. . . . [29]

Dr. Kempin also taught a course in Roman law at the University of New York. Turned down for a full-time post, in 1891 she returned to Switzerland to teach full-time at the University of Berne.[30] Now well established, the adult education program she helped establish continued to grow, becoming part of NYU's Division of General Education in 1934.

By the third year of the program, more than fifty women were enrolled in each class. Rumors spread that the women were becoming lawyers, but the Women's Legal Education Society did not offer a law degree. It was true, however, that almost every woman who went on to study for the law had attended classes in the makeshift Greenwich Village schoolroom.

There was a nearby place for them to study law without leaving home. The University of New York Law School began admitting women in 1890. The Women's Legal Education Society raised money for scholarships to the law school. The prize went to winners of an essay contest. Many of the women who went on to graduate from the University of New York Law School volunteered time to the society to help other poor immigrant women. Just about all of them devoted their careers to helping other less fortunate people.

The first three women graduates of the University of New York Law School were Melle Stanleyetta Titus, Cornelia Kelley Hood, and Katherine Hogan. Titus, New York City's first woman lawyer, enrolled in 1891. She graduated with high honors, and in a few years became the first woman admitted to the U.S. District Court for the Southern District of New York as well as the Second Circuit Court of Appeals. She continued to give free time to the Women's Legal Education Society.

Cornelia Kelley Hood worked for the Legal Aid Society and Consumers League and set up law classes for Brooklyn women. Katherine Hogan specialized in labor law and worked for a citywide association of women teachers, engaged in a struggle to win the same pay scale as the male teachers. Hogan was later credited for pioneering the idea of "Equal Pay for Equal Work."[31]

In 1893, the year of Myra Bradwell's death, the Chicago Columbian Exposition (World's Fair) became a symbolic battleground between the new back-to-the-kitchen forces, women's rights advocates, and African Americans. At the entrance to the fairgrounds, black men and women handed out leaflets entitled "The Reason Why the Colored American is not in the World's Columbian Exposition." Frederick Douglass had initiated the protest when fair organizers banned an exhibit on the accomplishments of African Americans. As president of the first black women's club in Chicago, Ida B. Wells had initiated a fund-raising project to pay for the brochures.[32]

Inside the fairgrounds, women milled about to see a scientific kitchen exhibit, demonstrating the new world of cooking appliances, stoves, and refrigerators. Women lawyers, including Phoebe Couzins, the first woman graduate of Washington University Law School in St. Louis, Missouri, had a small table at the Women's Pavilion with information on the accomplishments of professional women. She was reportedly upset by the lack of interest in the pioneering work of women lawyers.

In 1895, Couzins and several graduates of the Women's Legal Education Society formed an Alumnae Association to encourage other women to study law. Couzins gave the opening speech, making no effort to conceal her anger:

> And I tell you young ladies that when you get into the realm of the law you will discover . . . that

man has been trying to do the housekeeping in the Temple of Justice for years . . . all by himself, with the result of cobwebs all over the place. . . . Legal fiction is piled upon legal fiction and precedent on precedent until the whole storehouse of law is in a helpless confused condition. It needs women's wit, women's fairness and women's sense of right and righteousness to put the legal fabric in order and repair.[33]

Her anger flowed from a real concern. Despite all of the work of the pioneer women lawyers, during that same year of 1895 four out of five law schools were still refusing to allow women to study, no matter what their qualifications.

Even in the nation's capital, where new jobs in law firms opened every year, women had made little progress. Delia Sheldon Jackson, a Wellesley graduate, whose father was superintendent of education for Alaska, could not find a law school willing to accept her. Since it was still possible to study for the bar without a legal degree, Jackson asked Ellen Spencer Mussey, a woman lawyer who had graduated from Howard University, to allow her to study in her small office. Mussey offered to form a women's law class if Jackson could find two other interested women.

The following year the Women's Law Class held its first session, taught by Mussey and another Washington attorney, Emma Gillett. Gillett had studied with Belva Lockwood and then also graduated from Howard in 1883. Three years later Mussey and Gilbert encouraged their students to push for admission to Columbian College in the nation's capital. The trustees refused to even interview the women. So Mussey and Gillett created the first women's school of law, Washington College of Law. Three of the seven trustees were sympathetic men. Mussey was named as the only

81

woman dean of a law school in the world. In the spring of 1899, six women received their law degrees.

Despite this small victory for women in law, their numbers had increased very little. They remained in the backwaters of society, still the "other." At a graduation speech at the East Florida Seminary for Women in Gainesville, Florida, in 1898, Judge Horatio Davis expressed what was still the generally accepted attitude toward women when he said, "Seek to be good, but aim not to be great. A woman's noblest station is retreat."[34]

4

"RARE BIRDS"

*Men have accused the woman lawyer of being
a failure . . . because she has not grown rich in
the practice of law, and that in the short space
of twenty years. The man's standards again—
the acquisition of wealth and power. I would
say to these accusers the aim of the woman
lawyer is not so much the acquisition of money
as to make an impression in the laws of this
country as will benefit the whole race. . . .*

—*Attorney Mary Lilly,
shortly before World War I* [1]

A prominent leader of the bar, Theon G. Strong, wrote
in his 1914 memoirs: "It is now more than thirty
years since Mrs. Lockwood was admitted, and the right
of women to practice was established, but I have never
yet seen a woman plead a case of any kind in court . . . and
I think it may be safely asserted that there is no prospect
that women will be seen except as a rara avis [rare bird]
in the ranks of the legal fraternity."[2]

Strong's observation turned out to be all too accu-
rate. Until the early 1960s women continued to com-
pose only from 1 to 3 percent of the legal profession.[3]
Yet despite the bleak outlook, after women won the
right to vote in 1919, a few intrepid souls continued to
try to practice law. They faced similar hardships to

those encountered by the earliest pioneer women lawyers. Colleges accepted only token numbers of women, and jobs remained difficult to find once women passed the bar.

In the first decades of the 1900s, it was still possible to take the bar examination without attending law school. Lyda Burton Conley, the first Native American woman lawyer in the United States, did just that. It was not the dream of a career that motivated her to bury her nose in dry law books but the need to educate herself for an ugly legal battle on behalf of her people.[4]

Conley was a child when her tribe, the Wyandot, arrived in Kansas and were soon almost exterminated by a smallpox epidemic. Three hundred people died, including Conley's mother. The survivors buried their dead in an Indian burial ground at Huron Park.

In 1904, Lyda Conley and her sister Lena learned that Congress had authorized the destruction of the Huron Park Indian Cemetery to make way for commercial buildings, a project favored by most of the influential people in Kansas City. The Conley sisters built a small shack in the burial grounds and erected a fence around the area, arming themselves and staying put. The local press nicknamed the area "Fort Conley," as fences were pulled down and the sisters quickly raised them up again.

Lyda Conley later told reporters that two large American flags were always close at hand. "In the event of the troops putting in an appearance, we had decided to wrap the folds of the flag around us, and tell the boys in blue to shoot."

Realizing that in the long run only legal proceedings would stop the government plan, Conley studied law books, prepared a case, and went to court. When the highest state court refused to grant an injunction to stop the bulldozers, Conley appealed to the U.S. Supreme Court, presenting a sixty-nine-page legal brief.

84

Newspapers covered the story closely. It had all of the ingredients that made headlines: two Indian women holed up with guns; dead bodies about to be disturbed. When reporters asked Conley why she didn't hire a lawyer, she said, "No lawyer could plead for the grave of my mother as I could; no lawyer could have the heart interest in the case that I have."

When they asked her if she thought she had a chance of winning, the reply came back, "If I do not then there is no cemetery in this land safe from sale." The Supreme Court refused to hear the case, but the courage of the two sisters drew so much support and attention that in 1912 the House of Representatives Indian Affairs committee banned desecration of the cemetery.

Lyda Conley passed the bar in 1910, but she never earned a living from legal work. She refused to defend anyone whom she believed to be guilty, except an Indian.

As the nation continued industrializing at breakneck speed, the small existing public school system could not absorb all the new immigrant children. Reformers called for "Americanization" through education, and the public school system grew rapidly. Naturally, teachers were needed. Since women were virtually barred from other professions, they crowded into short-term teacher training courses and found jobs in thousands of new schools.

By 1911, women, most of them native born, composed 78 percent of all public school teachers. But only a few young immigrant women could obtain enough education to qualify as grade school teachers, let alone attend college. In 1905, among the millions of new Eastern European immigrants in New York City, more than half the young men and three quarters of the young women were employed in "manual trades." In many families, the daughters went to work in the garment shops and one or two sons attended a state university or tuition-free City College in New York City. A few evening colleges opened in some cities to accommodate full-time working men.

Most men of the legal world continued to exclude women from "their" profession, but there were always a few good men who bucked the tide.[5] In 1902, Alice Dillingham was attending an all-women's college, Bryn Mawr. She listened as the dean of the New York University Law School, Clarence Ashley, urged Bryn Mawr seniors to study law. Most of the women, knowing how almost no jobs existed for them in the world of law, did not respond. Dillingham was the only recruit in her class. She graduated from NYU Law School in 1905 as class valedictorian.

Six years later, in 1908, Portia Law School, the only all-women's law school in the world, opened in Boston. It started out as an evening bar examination review course taught by a male Boston attorney, Arthur W. MacLean. Portia grew quickly and was permitted to grant bachelor of law degrees to women by 1919.[6] Three quarters of Portia's students were the children and grandchildren of immigrants—Irish, Jewish, and Italian. The rest were from poor New England families of English and Scottish descent.

Other short-lived experiments with all-women's law schools were attempted, but only Portia endured. In 1915, Elizabeth Chadwick Beale was rejected by Harvard Law School despite the fact that her father, Joseph H. Beale, was a law professor there. She persuaded her father to open a law school for graduates of elite women's colleges. Twenty-five graduates of Radcliffe, Bryn Mawr, and Smith applied, and Professor Beale convinced several other law professors to take on teaching assignments. Despite its self-promotion as "the only graduate law school for women in the United States" (since Portia did not require a college degree), the school folded after one year when Elizabeth Beale married and changed her mind about studying the law.

At just about the same time that Portia opened its doors, women's medical schools were closing. In a move to further "professionalize" medicine, the Carnegie Foundation hired Abraham Flexner to judge the quality of medical schools. The Flexner Report of 1910 claimed that women's institutions were no longer needed since other schools were accepting women. But this was not true. As the ranks of applicants to medical schools swelled, many women were turned away.[7]

With laws varying from state to state, the standardization of law education requirements took longer than medical ones. The prejudice against female lawyers, especially trial lawyers, remained firmly in place.

In 1914, a woman lawyer wrote to the editor of the *New York Sun*:

> When the girl lawyer tries her first case, the jury will smile affably upon her and so perhaps will the Judge, but there is one person who will not smile and that is the opposing counsel who objects to a woman adversary. . . . She knows that he is thinking that she has no place in the courtroom; if she is a good-looking girl she's out to be married; if she isn't good-looking she ought to be dead or else justifying her existence by serving in the capacity of an overworked stenographer to some dignified member of the nobler sex.

Clarice Baright, a New York lawyer, was interviewed by a *New York World* reporter in 1916. He asked her if women lawyers won their cases by flirting. "I've never known a woman lawyer who got anything except by hard work," she retorted angrily.[8]

Women trial lawyers continued to defend indigent clients who had nowhere else to turn. Tiera Farrow became famous in 1915 when her client, Clara Schweiger, during a divorce action, pulled out a gun in the courthouse and shot her husband. Farrow represented her during her subsequent murder trial, the first time a woman lawyer in Missouri ever tried a murder case. Farrow mounted an impressive defense, and Schweiger was found guilty of the lesser charge of manslaughter.

As usual, the press, instead of commenting on Farrow's talents in the court, emphasized her physical appearance. One reporter wrote:

> Miss Tiera Farrow, young, good-looking and most feminine in appearance—not at all the sort of person one would connect with the wrangling of attorneys and the heated debates usually attendant upon murder trials.[9]

Ten years later, when Farrow and a few colleagues were teaching women's law classes in Kansas City, the *Kansas City Star*, apparently not checking on Farrow's legal background, commented that women have not what is loosely called a legal mind.

Only a handful of women were appointed to the bench, usually in the lowest-ranking assignments as justice of the peace, temporary probate judge, or minor posts in tiny country courthouses. The few who made it into more prominent spots were almost always assigned to "women's judgeships"—in divorce courts and juvenile courts. Women lawyers talked about struggling for more judicial appointments, but most agreed that this would not happen until they achieved some political power through the vote. But NAWSA members, demoralized by the failures of the state-by-state campaigns, had long since decided that continued education was their only recourse.

After Susan B. Anthony's death in 1906, Carrie Chapman Catt took over the reins of the half-alive suffrage struggle when she returned to New York City after twenty years in England. Joining forces with Harriot Stanton Blatch, Elizabeth Cady Stanton's daughter, she formed the Equality League of Self-Supporting Women, later called the Women's Political Union. By 1908, the League had 19,000 members, including dynamic trade union leaders like Rose Schneiderman, a garment worker, and women of the burgeoning settlement house movement. They campaigned vigorously against state assemblymen opposed to suffrage.[10]

In 1909, the Woman Suffrage Party, dedicated to more militant tactics, was launched. Catt decided to stick with NAWSA and build support for forthcoming referendums. At the 1910 NAWSA convention there were heated debates over tactics and strategies for victory. Many women were convinced that the referenda were useless.

Women lawyers participated in the suffrage movement. In 1913, on the day before Woodrow Wilson's inauguration as president, the capital overflowed with visitors. When Wilson arrived, the streets were empty. Thousands of people were over on Pennsylvania Avenue watching a spectacular NAWSA show.

Five thousand women were marching down the street. They had received a police permit for their demonstration, but when the women were threatened by hundreds of wild-eyed supporters of "femininity," the police were unable to control the fray. Federal troops were brought to the scene to reinforce the police, as the bullies continued rushing into the street to break up the columns of women marchers. Male students from Maryland Agricultural College arranged themselves single file around the marchers to form a human barrier against their attackers. The women continued to march, heads held high.

Carrie Chapman Catt was a leader of the women's suffrage struggle.

One twenty-year-old woman, Katherine Robinson Everett, watched the march and heard the later speeches and decided then and there to study law when she saw

> all those beautiful and talented women lawyers from New York marching for suffrage. . . . They were so eloquent, so impressive, and they talked about using the law to deal with human rights and human problems. They made it clear that being a lawyer wasn't just a job, it was a way of bringing about important changes in society. I don't think I will ever forget the day I saw that suffrage march.[11]

The public was shocked by the spectacle of men attacking women, and the Washington chief of police eventually lost his job. Dozens of delegations visited the new president with stacks of petitions urging him to back suffrage.

Petitions and marches still did not win the vote. Alice Paul, a Quaker social worker who had participated in the militant British suffrage movement, returned home to the United States in 1910. A few months after the Washington march, the Congressional Union announced its formation, headed by Paul, and began publishing a weekly newspaper. NAWSA thought any talk of an all-out push for an equal rights amendment was premature.

In 1914 a wealthy supporter died, leaving Catt over $2 million to be used expressly for the suffrage fight. NAWSA poured money into campaigns in Massachusetts, Pennsylvania, and New Jersey but still went down in defeat. At that point NAWSA's demoralized forces were shrinking. The Congressional Union, with far less money, stepped up their work for a constitutional amendment, with or without President Wilson's support.

In time for the 1916 presidential campaign, the Congressional Union opposed the reelection of Wilson while NAWSA endorsed his candidacy. NAWSA members were elated when Wilson and his wife appeared at NAWSA's convention in September 1916. The president made no promises, but he hinted broadly about possible support for women's voting rights.

The suffrage struggle was thoroughly covered in the press, but only African American–owned newspapers and a few socialist publications championed the rights of minorities. Blacks and Latinos worked at the hardest and lowest-paying jobs. Except for the rapidly growing Industrial Workers of the World (IWW), known as the "Wobblies," most unions barred them from membership.

William E. B. DuBois, an African American sociologist and one of the very few black men who had earned a Ph.D., became the undisputed leader of the Niagara Movement, an early civil rights organization. After a bloody race riot in 1908 in Springfield, Illinois, DuBois called the members of his Niagara group together early in 1909. A number of prominent white leaders joined with them to form the National Association for the Advancement of Colored People (NAACP). The NAACP would take the leadership in the struggle for civil rights until the 1960s.

In the early 1900s, 95 percent of the nation's almost 9 million African Americans still lived in the South, many of them tenant farmers and sharecroppers barely able to feed their families. After World War I broke out in Europe in 1914, factory owners, shut off from Europe's immigrant labor supply, sent recruiters south. African American newspapers in Chicago and New York urged black Southerners to make "the Flight Out of Egypt." From 1915 until the late 1920s a million and a half African Americans heeded their call and became part of the "Great Migration" to Detroit, Chicago, and New York City.

Life in the northern cities was an improvement but no picnic. Housing and job discrimination were rigidly in place. African Americans, poorly educated and many of them skilled only in farmwork, suffered from under-employment and unemployment. Many poor whites resented the new competition for slum housing and unskilled jobs. Race riots broke out over the years in several cities, the most violent in East St. Louis.

Black women worked as domestics in middle-class and wealthy homes or did piecework as seamstresses and tailors in their homes. A tiny group of better-off black women managed to attend black colleges like Howard University and one or two other schools in the East and Midwest, and even they often could get jobs only as domestics. African American women saw little point in pushing for a role in the legal profession. With white women lawyers so few and far between, after all, and black men finding the odds almost insurmountable, what chance would a black woman have?[12]

The "findings" of "learned scholars" especially reinforced racism against black women. For example, Howard Washington Odum, in his much publicized Columbia University doctoral dissertation, "The Social and Mental Traits of the Negro," insisted that the "Negro woman . . . fails to assist the men in a better struggle, she is inefficient and indisposed to be faithful. She is a hindrance to the saving of money and the industrial development of the family."[13]

With racism on the rise in the North, the American Bar Association had actually admitted three black male lawyers by 1912, apparently because their race had not been known when they applied. The ABA quickly announced that it would be necessary to list racial categories on every application.

In 1914, a popular magazine for lawyers, *Case and Comment*, devoted an entire issue to the "new woman lawyer." The magazine published a racist "joke" about

93

a "mammy" wandering stupefied into a courtroom but made no reference to black women attorneys, not even to Charlotte E. Ray.

In 1918, only one black woman lawyer, Gertrude E. Rush, was known to exist. More than twenty years later, in the 1940s, only fifty-seven African American women nationally were lawyers (see Chapter 6).

In early 1917, with America's entry into World War I seemingly unavoidable, Carrie Chapman Catt and other leaders of NAWSA, disgusted with President Wilson's vacillation, decided to elevate the struggle for women's suffrage "to the position of a crusade for human freedom."[14] Alice Paul's Congressional Union had given up on marches and petitions and instead, in bitter cold weather, picketed outside the White House gates. NAWSA publicly criticized this tactic.

On April 2, 1917, the United States declared war on Germany. World War I caused a rift in the ranks of the suffrage movement, the labor movement, and the black civil rights movement that never truly healed. Carrie Chapman Catt jumped in to support the war, believing that if women contributed to the war effort they would no longer be denied the vote. Alice Paul's forces disagreed. W. E. B. DuBois publicly supported the war, hoping that if African Americans helped "save the world for democracy," as President Wilson proclaimed, black men would be included as recipients of the new democratic spirit.[15]

But black men quickly discovered that they were not welcome in the segregated armed forces. Only a few spaces were open to them in all-black army contingents, under the command of white officers.

The government launched a campaign to make support for the war an issue of patriotism. War rallies were held everywhere, with pretty young women urging young men to jump up on the stage with them and volunteer to serve in the bloody conflict raging overseas.

The Espionage Act of 1917 and the Sedition Act of 1918 were designed to prevent those who opposed the war from speaking out—and to harass trade unionists, especially the Wobblies, who opposed the war as "a rich man's war."

In the middle of the disputes about World War I, there was little unity when police raided union and political meetings on the Lower East Side and arrested several leaders who had not yet attained citizenship. Hasty proceedings were initiated, and many were ordered deported. On September 5, 1917, a mass sweep arrest was made on Wobbly headquarters throughout the nation. Thousands were deported.

Most lawyers stayed far away from these controversial cases. But in the state of Washington, when seventy-four IWW (Wobbly) leaders were put on trial on false murder charges, Caroline Lowe joined the defense team. She had been admitted to the Kansas bar only a year earlier and was secretary of the Socialist Party's women's national committee. Despite the inflammatory atmosphere of the time, she helped to win a not-guilty verdict for the accused labor leaders and then raced off to Chicago, where over 100 Wobbly organizers, including William ("Big Bill") Haywood, the IWWs best-known and best-loved leader, had been moved for a trial that lasted five months. Once again Caroline Lowe sat at the defense table. By then the Great Red Scare (calling labor leaders "communists") had moved into high gear, and the jury's guilty verdict was no surprise.

Caroline Lowe continued to fight for her labor clients, as well as immigrants threatened with deportation because of their political or antiwar beliefs. She was present to defend them at Ellis Island in New York City, saving some of them from last-minute deportations. She then rushed back to Kansas for the trial of twenty-five more Wobblies in Wichita. For the rest of her life she worked for labor causes.

Conscientious objectors, socialists, and just plain folks who opposed the war were attacked on the streets and saw their homes and headquarters raided. But among the earliest victims of the wartime campaign against free speech were the women who stood in front of the White House holding banners that read "Democracy Should Begin at Home" and referring to the President as "Kaiser Wilson." The women were attacked by mobs of snarling men.

On June 22, 1917, the women were arrested but their attackers were not. Since the Constitution's Bill of Rights guaranteed their right to wave any banners they cared to lift aloft, the cases against them were at first dismissed. But as the war fever escalated and the women continued to demonstrate, they were, one by one, given increasingly long jail sentences.[16]

Ninety-seven of these women were sent to prison, some of them to Occoquan Workhouse in nearby Virginia, where conditions were notoriously bad. The women initiated a hunger strike to protest their illegal arrests and were force-fed, turning them into national martyrs. Among the prisoners were many professional women as well as working-class women.

Carrie Chapman Catt and others in NAWSA publicly announced that their organization opposed these actions. In suffrage parades some women actually carried signs condemning the women in jail. More picketers replaced the jailed women in front of the White House and, despite NAWSA's lack of solidarity, protests poured in from around the nation as the imprisoned women grew more and more ill and skeletal.

Shortly after a senator visited the Occoquan Workhouse, a report favoring women's suffrage emerged from a Senate committee. The House of Representatives scheduled a vote on the Anthony Amendment for January 10, 1918. Under a wave of public protest, the hunger strikers were freed at the end of November 1917.

In March 1918 the Washington, D.C., Court of Appeals reversed their convictions.

In later years the Woman's Party took credit for Congress's finally voting in favor of women's suffrage. NAWSA insisted that women's involvement in war work during the brief period of America's involvement in World War I had turned the tide.

It is hard to judge exactly which approach moved more politicians—the embarrassment caused by the women hunger strikers or the well-publicized war efforts of NAWSA women—but all through 1917, by means of voluntary legislative action and victorious referenda, several states granted women the vote.[17]

Right before the scheduled vote in the House of Representatives on January 10, 1918, President Wilson announced that he supported women's suffrage. All polls showed that the vote would be painfully close. A two-thirds majority was required in both houses of Congress to pass a constitutional amendment. Once again woman activists depended on a few good men to make the difference. Four congressional supporters of suffrage were too ill to participate in the debates, but they showed up for the vote—one on a stretcher! The wife of Representative Hicks of New York, an ardent supporter of suffrage, died right before the final tally was taken. Hicks showed up for the count and then returned home to bury his life companion. The two-thirds majority was achieved by such a close squeak that the women watching from the gallery thought they had lost until cheers from their supporters came from the chamber below.[18]

In June of 1919, the Senate also approved women's suffrage. Then, as required by the Constitution, three-fourths of the states, through legislative action or special conventions, ratified the nineteenth Amendment. On August 18, 1920, women were finally granted voting rights.

In 1918 women gained President Wilson's support
for their right to vote.

Despite the victory, twenty-seven law schools continued to refuse to enroll the newly enfranchised "second sex," including Columbia University and, the most resistant of all, Harvard. Yale was the exception, finally permitting a few token women to enter its law school—one in 1918 and five in 1919. More than forty years later, Matilda Fenberg recalled the isolation of those days from the moment she registered—when shouts of "fire, fire" rang through the halls. Fenberg graduated in 1922 and established a successful law practice in Chicago.

Most people continued to have more to worry about. When World War I ended in 1919, millions were thrown out of work and wages were cut for many still clinging to their jobs. The labor movement responded with strikes. The Federal Bureau of Investigation (FBI) was created, with J. Edgar Hoover heading it up to keep check on "Reds" and labor leader "troublemakers." With job competition increasing, racism against African Americans escalated again. More than two dozen cities, including the nation's capital, experienced bloody race riots during the "Red Summer" of 1919, as police and troops once more protected white attackers.

W. E. B. DuBois declared an "unbending battle against the forces of hell in our land."[19] But the government struck first. In 1920 it launched Attorney General A. Mitchell Palmer's "Red Scare." Police and FBI agents conducted surprise raids without search warrants on homes and meeting halls. In the New York State legislature, five elected Socialist members were denied their seats. Within a few weeks, not only was the Socialist Party barely in existence but a pall of silence hung over all reform movements.

All of these events heartened the "nativists," those who had been ranting against immigrants since the nineteenth century. In 1920 the influential pioneer automobile manufacturer Henry Ford filled the pages of his newspaper, the *Dearborn Independent*, with a full-scale racist attack on Jewish Americans, especially those involved in the labor movement. Threatened by a lawsuit and a boycott of automobiles, Ford eventually apologized, but the damage had been done.

Many universities, especially the elite institutions, turned away Jewish applicants, no matter how excellent their credentials. Most simply set up secret quota systems, limiting Jewish admissions to near zero. Harvard, however, publicly announced its intentions to allow fewer Jewish students into its classes.

In 1924, Congress passed new immigration laws that established a quota system by country of origin. This quota system, which favored immigrants from white, Christian countries of northwestern Europe, lasted until it was eliminated by the influence of the Civil Rights Movement of the 1960s.

Meanwhile, as minorities and immigrants suffered, a sizable privileged middle class developed as industrialization almost doubled and the introduction of new technologies leaped forward. Household appliances, refrigerators, stoves, even washing machines became widely available, and a so-called "new woman," considerably freed of household tasks, emerged. The advertising business expanded to push the sales of the new miracle appliances. Equating their clients' products with liberty and freedom for women, one company hailed its toaster as "The Toaster that FREED 456,000 HOMES . . . from ever watching, turning or burning toast."[20]

Taking advantage of the new postsuffrage "feminist" spirit, the owner of the American Tobacco Company hired a publicist, Edward Bernays, to improve the tarnished image of women who smoked cigarettes. When a consulting psychologist declared that "women regard cigarettes as symbols of freedom,"[21] Bernays organized a contingent of women in the 1929 Easter Parade, who marched along "lighting their 'torches of freedom' . . . as a protest against woman's inequality."[22] Within half a century, women were moving quickly toward "equality" with men in a less desired department—lung cancer!

The majority of middle-class women stayed home, keeping house and raising families with their new appliances and—for the more affluent—the help of black and immigrant servants. Others, however, continued to struggle for interesting and fulfilling careers, including those in the legal profession. Now that the vote had been won, there was not even a remnant of a women's rights movement to press for equality for working women. Professional organizations like the National Association of Women Lawyers had little power in the male-dominated field of law. Women lawyers lucky enough to find work continued to face barriers in all fields except for a few openings in the areas of poverty law and family law, and in a sprinkling of lower-status government jobs.

The percentage of women in the legal profession grew at a snail's pace and then stopped growing completely after the stock market crash of 1929 and the subsequent ten years of the Great Depression. Without the part-time law schools then available, it would have been impossible for many men and just about all women to study for the law. Full-time schools not only cost three or four times the tuition of the part-time ones, but most working women could not find time to fulfill the requirement of a college degree from an accredited school. Even women with college educations were turned away from many of the full-time law schools.

It was no secret that despite the supposed superiority of the high-priced colleges, the part-time students, so many of them immigrants and women, had to pass the same bar examinations taken by Ivy League law graduates. Leaders of the bar, most of them corporation lawyers, were upset when reports showed that the scores of the part-timers were as good or better than those of the Ivy League graduates and that the number of foreign-born lawyers was increasing.[23] They viewed the part-time schools as havens for aliens, foreign-born citizens, and U.S.-born members of ethnic minority groups, as well as women. Led by the Association of American Law Schools, the American Bar Association, and Harvard's prominent dean, Roscoe Pound, the elite fought to raise the admission requirements to the bar to such high levels that the daughters and sons of immigrants and the poor would be eliminated from the competition. Oral bar exams were added to the requirements in Massachusetts and several other states. Seeing the applicants in person made it easier to identify and eliminate the "unacceptable."

The part-time law schools survived the assault. In 1934, when legal jobs were scarce during the hard economic times, the Supreme Judicial Court of Massachusetts ruled that two years of college training prior to law school were required in order to be permitted to take the bar examination. Portia and Suffolk quickly established a junior college. Until 1938, Portia remained the only all women's law school in the nation. But that year, with enrollments declining, Portia admitted men. At the school's peak, in 1929, about 30 percent of all women law students in the United States had attended Portia.

Gradually the feminist-led Washington College of Law changed. In 1929 the school opened a small day session, upgraded its curriculum, and raised its tuition fees. It lost some working-class students and gained a few from the middle class who had been turned away by more prestigious institutions. In the 1929–30 academic year, its 271 students, less than half the number at Portia, came from homes in forty-two states and ten foreign countries. Only one out of three were women, most of them middle class, and very few of them second- or third-generation ethnics. Despite the changes in their

102

own student body, Washington's administration joined Portia and Suffolk in opposing Dean Pound's efforts to eliminate the night colleges. As the Depression continued until the end of the 1930s, Portia's enrollments dropped and Washington College of Law's increased. By then the student body was three-quarters male.

People could still take the bar examination in some places without law school training, but the law had become so much more complex that it was not practical to attempt it. It was extremely difficult for women *with* law degrees to find work. Without one it was just about impossible, and *where* the degree was obtained was also very important.

Women who graduated from full-time coed law schools were first in line to obtain the few law-related jobs available for women. During the Depression, some women lawyers worked in the government's New Deal programs, but most were relegated to clerical jobs. Only a handful were promoted by government agencies to junior or senior attorney spots.

Very few Portia women were able to earn a full-time living in the law profession. Boston University women graduates did a little better. About 150 of them worked full-time during the 1920s and 1930s, some in law offices or government jobs. Others, like Emma Fall Schofield, taught law part-time at Boston University and Portia. But the women graduates were never as successful as the men graduated from the same institution.

Charlotte Slavitt's experience was fairly typical of Boston University's graduates of the twenties and thirties. The daughter of Ukrainian immigrants, she was one of only fifteen women in the school in the mid-1920s. Many of them were Jewish, some of whom were turned away by other institutions because of bias. Most Protestants stayed away from schools with high percentages of students from immigrant families. Slavitt passed the bar and moved to Chicago. Rebuffed by law firms, she opened her own office during the Depression. Most of her clients were penniless, referred to her by judges or prison inmates and guards. Slavitt barely scraped by, but she gained enormous experience.

As in Charlotte Slavitt's case, defending the poor—which was called "poverty law"—provided the majority of jobs for women attorneys.[24] Some women certainly worked in this field because other jobs were unobtainable, but many women, then as well as later when other fields opened to them, chose this work because of their concern for social justice.

Before World War I, churches, social clubs, labor's "mutual aid" societies, and a few wealthy philanthropists raised "charity" money to help those who would otherwise starve to death. From 1910 on, reformers and Progressive Party activists pushed state legislatures to provide pensions for widows with children and "general assistance" for those unable to work.

By 1920, with poverty an ever-pressing and ever-growing concern, state legislatures passed hundreds of new public welfare laws and a large bureaucracy grew to administer the laws. As the Great Depression sent millions more tumbling into poverty, the number of "home relief" (welfare) recipients rose dramatically. The amount of money given to the poor was barely enough to keep the flame of life burning.

President Herbert Hoover adamantly refused to involve the federal government in the problem. But his successor, Franklin Delano Roosevelt, who had won the presidency with the votes of working people, pushed Congress to appropriate $500 million for relief shortly after he took office in 1933. His administration established work programs to provide jobs. By 1934, 28 million people, more than 22 percent of the population, were dependent on these programs for their daily bread.[25]

Growing numbers of people with legal problems did not have money to pay for the promised "equal justice."

The system of court-appointed attorneys that Clara Foltz had innovated failed completely as fewer and fewer lawyers were willing to work for token wages. The Legal Aid Society had offered free legal assistance to poor people since the 1880s, but it did not have the facilities to deal with the expanded numbers of people needing help.

In a 1919 report, "Justice and the Poor," Reginald Heber Smith, a prominent Boston attorney, had summed up the obvious:

> The administration of American justice is not impartial, the rich and the poor do not stand on an equality before the law, [and] the traditional method of providing justice . . . has caused a gross denial of justice in all parts of the country to millions of persons.[26]

In 1934, during a speech at the University of Michigan Law School, Supreme Court justice Harlan F. Stone sharply criticized the legal profession for its profound interest in corporations and lack of involvement with ordinary people. He claimed that "the learned profession of an earlier day" had become "the obsequious servant of business."[27]

His much publicized speech drew the support of several law professors and lawyers. A movement for "Legal Realism" emerged, that was sharply critical of corporate law firms. Many supporters of this movement worked in New Deal agencies and pushed for the passage of the Social Security Act of 1935.

Despite their work, little changed for poor defendants. The National Lawyers Guild attempted a small-scale legal services program in 1938, but the guild was never able to raise enough money to meet the increasing need.

The shortage of personnel was a major problem at Legal Aid offices. The original plan had been to staff

Legal Aid with young male lawyers looking for experience, but except for some Jewish law school graduates who could not find employment in law firms, most men avoided the stigma and low pay associated with poverty law. Women lawyers became the backbone of poverty law services.

But even at Legal Aid societies, women almost never worked in the criminal division. Throughout the twenties and thirties, women were still seldom seen in courtrooms. Tiera Farrow was told not to take criminal law classes at Kansas City School of Law. A judge ordered Margaret Hickey to leave the courtroom when any discussion of rape took place. Women lawyers were caught in a real contradiction. It was considered improper for them to defend criminals, but "proper" areas of the law, like corporation law and the settling of estates, were maintained as a male preserve.

Only a tiny group of women lawyers with male friends or relatives in high places found jobs in private law firms. In 1924, Wall Street hired a woman believed to be its first female associate, Catherine Noyes Lee, a magna cum laude graduate of NYU Law School and the daughter of a prominent judge. During the Depression, Helen L. Buttenweiser, the niece of New York's governor Herbert Lehman, found a job in a Wall Street firm but by 1937 moved to the Legal Aid Society in New York as chair of its board of directors.

Although there were many women in her class of 1933, Buttenweiser later said that "people thought there had to be something terribly mannish and aggressive about you if you planned to study law." When one of the students was obviously pregnant, the professors "actually went so far as to hold a vote as to whether it was improper for a young man to be in contact with a pregnant woman."[28]

Until very recent times, pregnancy was viewed as a barrier to public appearances of any kind. During one delayed murder trial in 1926, Bessie R. Geffner, the lawyer for the defense, was expecting a baby. The courtroom was hot, but she wore a large overcoat to disguise her condition. The judge noticed anyway and ordered her out of the courtroom.

A small group of women lawyers ignored the unwritten rules of the game. California's Gladys Towles Root apparently agreed with the old adage that it was better to be hung for a fox than a sheep. Since women were insulted even when they dressed conservatively and behaved unaggressively in the courtroom, apparently Root decided that the best way to counter the unofficial regulations was to break all of them. Making a name for herself as a specialist in sex crimes, she defied many other courtroom codes that had nothing to do with the law. She often dyed her hair to match bright-colored garish costumes. "I should have joined a circus," she once commented. Her daring courtroom tactics and often brilliant defense work made her famous. A jingle of the time proclaimed:

Root-de-toot, toot-de-toot
Here's to Gladys Towles Root,
Her dresses are purple, her hats are wide,
She'll get you one instead of five.

Root not only was an ardent feminist. She was also a firm opponent of racism. In 1931, she defended a young Filipino man prohibited by law from marrying his Caucasian girlfriend, challenging the constitutionality of the California statute. Her law firm handled more than 1,600 cases a year, winning an unusually high percentage of them. Commenting on the reactions of defeated opposing male attorneys, Root said:

Many a male lawyer when defeated by a woman
will blame it on that mystic factor they call

feminine intuition. That is his excuse. In plain language, he faced too much perception and intelligence and logical thinking.[29]

Mary Kaufman was more typical of activist women attorneys of that time. Born in 1912, she was raised in a poor family on the Lower East Side of New York and attended college during the Depression years. Her mother influenced her enormously, leading a rent strike and participating in hunger marches in the 1930s.

Kaufman earned her bachelor's degree in political science at Brooklyn College—which, like its sister school, the City College of New York (CCNY), was then tuition-free—and then attended night classes at St. John's Law School while holding a day job at a New Deal–created Works Progress Administration (WPA) project. Admitted to the bar in 1937, she became a Lawyers Guild activist. She worked for a labor lawyer for five dollars a week and then took a job with the New York State Labor Relations Board. There, she pressed charges against companies defying labor laws or interfering with union-organizing drives.

Only a handful of women were allowed to "mount the bench." Almost all of them were appointed to the juvenile courts and family courts. Often, these judges took it upon themselves to expand their work far beyond required courtroom duties.

Mary Margaret Bartelme, for example, who had been encouraged to study law years earlier by Myra Bradwell, served as a circuit court judge in the juvenile court system of Cook County, Illinois. In her "spare" time, Bartelme pioneered the creation of halfway houses for teenage girls, even using her own home. They called her "suitcase Mary," because no one ever left one of her homes without a valise packed with new clothes.[30]

One of the few female elected judges was Florence Ellinwood Allen, who graduated from NYU Law School in 1913. When the Nineteenth Amendment passed, Allen ran for a judgeship with the Court of Common Pleas in Cuyahoga County, Ohio, and became the first woman to win a judicial post through the ballot. When the male justices of the court attempted to limit her to divorce cases, she adamantly refused to accept this.

In 1922, Allen was elected to the Ohio Supreme Court and six years later won reelection by a 350,000-vote majority. In 1934, Franklin Delano Roosevelt appointed Allen to the United States Court of Appeals for the Sixth Circuit, again a first-time achievement by a woman. According to Allen, her male colleagues were horribly upset. One even took to his bed for a few days.

There was almost always protest from other judges and members of the bar when a woman was appointed to a judgeship. When Calvin Coolidge appointed Genevieve Rose Cline to the United States Customs Court in 1928, the New York Customs Bar Association put up a stiff fight against the appointment.

Women remained rara avises ("rare birds") on the bench until the 1970s. Even then they were a relatively small minority. But for a brief time in 1925, because of an odd circumstance, three women made up the Texas State Supreme Court! One of the parties in a famous land dispute, *Johnson* v. *Darr*, was the organization, the "Woodmen of the World." It turned out that just about every judge in the state held a membership card in the all-male organization. When the three male justices of the Supreme Court disqualified themselves, the governor of Texas appointed the first woman lawyer in Texas, Hortense Ward, as well as Ruth Brazzil and Hattie L. Heneberg, exciting the media all over the state.

After the case ended, not a single woman was appointed to a judgeship in Texas until 1934, when Sarah T. Hughes was appointed to a lower court. When Hughes was admitted to the bar in 1922, all she could find was a desk job answering the telephone and typing letters.

New York City had been one of the major centers for the suffrage, social reform, and labor movements, but it remained one of the most difficult places for a job-hunting woman attorney. As the world's financial center, it hosted an elite flock of Wall Street lawyers and national corporate law offices. Clara Foltz spent ten years there offering legal assistance to poor immigrant women. When she was plunged into poverty herself, she returned to the West Coast.

In 1910, at the age of sixty-one, Foltz became the first woman ever to be appointed deputy district attorney in Los Angeles. As president of the Los Angeles Votes for Women Club that year, she drafted a suffrage amendment. In 1930, still active at the age of eighty-one, she ran in the Republican Party primary for the governorship of California and polled 3,570 votes with her women's rights platform.

As always, there were a few good men in positions of power who tried to help women attorneys succeed. One of them was the mayor of New York, Fiorello LaGuardia, who advanced the careers of several women attorneys during his terms in office. The women lawyers did not disappoint him. Dorothy Kenyon was especially talented. Kenyon had passed the bar examination in 1917 and worked as a researcher for the government on labor and peace issues. Like so many other women lawyers, she had often expressed unpopular views, publicly stating many times that prostitutes were unfairly prosecuted while their pimps and customers went untouched by the law. In 1936 LaGuardia named Kenyon his first deputy commissioner of licenses, and in 1939 he appointed her to a judgeship in the municipal court.

Columbia University Law School, like Harvard, many of whose graduates went on to work for elite establishments, had long turned away women. One of the rejected women later insisted that Dean Harlan Fiske Stone was to blame for the stonewalling. "Everyone knew," she said, that "Harlan Stone promised women would be admitted to Columbia over his dead body."[31] Stone went on to become chief justice of the United States Supreme Court.

In 1927, another Columbia Law School dean finally submitted to pressure and lifted the ban on women. There was no word of Harlan Stone's collapsing on the capital steps, but some women claimed they sent him a sarcastic telegram asking if he had.

Admission was one thing, acceptance another. In Columbia's law classes, the men left empty seats around them and on a few occasions, when a woman student was called on to speak, "men stamped their feet so that her answer couldn't even be heard."[32] Harvard Law School continued to refuse to admit women all through the 1930s and 1940s.

A degree from an Ivy League college like Columbia held the promise of better job possibilities. Ida Klaus, for example, from a poor family in Brownsville, Brooklyn, made connections at Columbia that she never would have found if she had attended Portia or Boston University. In 1928, while she studied and worked part-time teaching Hebrew, she also became a research assistant to a supportive professor, Herman Oliphant, who brought her to Washington, D.C., when he was given a job by Roosevelt's New Deal government in 1933. Her talents were recognized, and she was soon on the road to a long and successful career.

Morris Ernst, a senior partner at a New York City law firm dedicated to civil liberties, Greenbaum, Wolff & Ernst, hired Harriet F. Pillpel, a 1935 graduate of Columbia Law School who had ranked second in her class. At that point, the sale of contraceptives was still banned by the Comstock Law. Pillpel was assigned to *Griswold* v. *Connecticut* in 1965, a case that eventually led to the striking down of the Comstock Law under the right-to-privacy interpretation of the Constitution.

It became an important precedent during the famous abortion rights case *Roe* v. *Wade* in 1973 (see Chapter 6). Pillpel drew many new clients to the firm, including birth control advocate Margaret Sanger and sexual behavior expert Alfred Kinsey, all admiring her for her work on behalf of women's reproductive rights.

Prejudice against women in the professions, especially those from immigrant backgrounds, persisted. Nonetheless, quite a few managed to slip through the cracks. But for African American and Latina women, racism remained a giant barrier to advancement.[33]

Although Latinas became schoolteachers, librarians, and nurses, there is no record of any Latina becoming a lawyer until 1961! Unlike African Americans who at least had a few universities concentrating on their education, Mexican Americans had nowhere to turn. They were excluded from most white campuses and for the most part attended segregated public schools. As unemployment rates skyrocketed in the 1930s, tens of thousands of Mexican immigrant workers were scapegoated for the problem. In the West and Midwest, they were herded into railroad freight cars and unceremoniously "dumped" in Mexico. Many of those deported were U.S. citizens![34]

Even after the civil rights legislation of the 1960s, when a few Latino men became lawyers, few Latinas did. Only in more recent times has this begun to change. Irma Vidal Santanella, born in 1924, is considered the pioneer Latina attorney (see Chapter 5). She did not even graduate from law school until 1961, almost a century later than the pioneer white women lawyers.[35]

African American women with an interest in the law profession, despite the few pioneers of earlier times, were starting out again from ground zero. A few of them from middle-class families managed to break the barriers in the 1920s and 1930s. Many—like Minneapolis lawyer Lena O. Smith, admitted to the Minnesota bar in 1921—devoted themselves to civil rights law, often through the NAACP.

Sadie Tanner Mossell Alexander, born in 1898 in Philadelphia, was the daughter of the first black American law school graduate. In 1924 she enrolled in the University of Pennsylvania Law School and graduated with top honors in 1927. She did not have fond memories of her time at the school. She described the dean as "a very prejudiced man." He

> directed that under no circumstances was I to be admitted to the club formed by the handful of women who attended the school at the time . . . so I would go home directly at twelve noon when classes were over and study alone until about six p.m. No one invited me to lunch—neither women nor men, so I just adapted myself to what was.[36]

Alexander's later work would bring her national recognition (see Chapter 5).

Violette N. Anderson, a graduate of Chicago Law School in 1920, became the first black woman admitted to the bar in Illinois. She went on to be the first woman assistant city prosecutor from 1922 through 1923; the first to serve as vice president of the Cook County Bar Association; and the first black woman admitted to practice before the U.S. Supreme Court.

Eunice Hunton Carter, probably the best-known of the black women attorneys of that period, earned her law degree at Fordham Law School in 1932 and was admitted to the New York bar in 1934. She considered herself lucky when district attorney William C. Dodge hired her to handle low-level prosecutions in the magistrate's (criminal) court. She had no inkling that her modest job would make her famous.

Eunice Hunton Carter, a well-known black woman
attorney in the 1930s in New York

Most of the cases Carter handled involved arrested prostitutes. Carter noticed a strange pattern emerging when the same bondsmen arrived to bail the women out and the same law firm sent the same lawyer, Abe Karp, to defend them. Karp was well-known as a Mafia lawyer. Carter approached Thomas E. Dewey, who had been appointed New York State special prosecutor in 1935, to look into organized crime. Dewey had planned to make loan sharks his main target. But convinced that Carter might be on the trail of something big, he hired her as the only black person *and* only woman on his famed "twenty against the underworld" team.

A full-scale investigation turned up the fact that Carter had been more than right. The underworld took in $12 million a year on prostitution alone during the Depression years, with Charles "Lucky" Luciano, New York's Mafia leader, in charge. The subsequent trial brought Luciano's conviction. It also brought Eunice Hunton Carter an appointment as chief of Dewey's Special Sessions Bureau, supervising more than 14,000 criminal cases each year.[37]

No matter how stellar their careers, black women attorneys knew that judgeships were pretty much out of their grasp. The first black woman judge in the United States was Jane Mathilda Bolin, appointed by Mayor LaGuardia as a justice in New York's Domestic Relations Court in 1939 (later called the Family Court).[38]

Edith S. Sampson, born in 1901, was the first black woman to be elected to a judgeship in the United States in 1962. She was one of the few black women from a less than well-off family who advanced in the legal profession. Always working for a living while attending schools, Sampson earned her Master of Law degree in 1927 at Loyola University, and was admitted to the Illinois bar. After a long combined career in social work and law, Sampson opened her own law office in the heart of Chicago's black neighborhood. If not for later

115

events on the world scene, she might have remained there throughout her life (see Chapter 5).

When the United States entered World War II in 1941, white women lawyers were still "rare birds" and black women lawyers even rarer. But they were often the only ones there for thousands of desperate poor people in need of legal help.

5

A JOKE THAT
CHANGED HISTORY

*If there were any need to prove your disrespect
you've already proved it by your laughter. We've
sat here for four days discussing the rights of
blacks and other minorities and there has been
no laughter, not even a smile. But when we sug-
gest that you shouldn't discriminate against your
own wives, your own mothers, your own grand-
daughters, your own sisters, then you laugh.*

*—Congresswoman Martha Griffiths,
debating the inclusion of an amendment
outlawing sex discrimination in Title VII
of the Civil Rights Act of 1964*[1]

*Better if Congress had just abolished sex itself.
A maid can now be a man. Girl Friday is an
intolerable offense. . . .*

—From a New York Times *editorial
ridiculing the inclusion of sex
discrimination in Title VII*[2]

The United States declared war on Japan after the
Japanese bombing of Pearl Harbor on December 7,
1941. And on December 11 Germany and Italy declared
war on the United States. As millions of men went off to

fight, women were urged to help the war effort by replacing men in the workplace. Three million women answered the call. Most took jobs in the war plants, building airplanes, tanks, and guns. Movie newsreels and the press glorified them as patriotic "Rosie the Riveter." Glamorous female movie stars posed for pictures dressed in overalls and goggles, like the symbolic "Rosie." Another 350,000 women joined the military. Articles in women's magazines written by psychologists who had always urged women to stay home to care for their children now claimed that children were better off when their mothers worked outside of the home.

In the professions some signs of change appeared. As enrollments dropped at medical schools and law schools, more women were educated to help maintain tuition income. With more male doctors needed in the war zones, this was especially true of medical schools. But the number of women enrolled in law schools also increased slightly during the war years,[3] and there were a few additional openings for women lawyers in small law firms, real estate offices, banks, and government agencies. Most of the women worked, as before, at desk jobs, but a few managed to find more exciting work.[4]

But within a year after the end of the war, as veterans came home and war industries slowed down, women were discharged from their jobs. Estimates were that 75 percent of them had planned to go on working. They had to content themselves with lower-paying clerical and sales jobs. Now psychologists claimed that juvenile delinquency was caused by mothers' working outside the home! Professional schools once again limited female applicants to the minimum, and the progress women made during World War II was quickly eroded. In the fall of 1946, a full-page advertisement signed by prominent women doctors protesting this situation appeared in the *New York Herald Tribune*. It was headlined "Doctors Wanted: No Women Need Apply."[5]

A few women lawyers attempted to defend the gains working women had achieved during the war. Anne Davidow, who had graduated from law school in 1920, agreed to represent Valentine Goesart in a case that eventually was heard before the Supreme Court. During the war, Valentine Goesart, the owner of a bar in Dearborn, Michigan, had hired two female employees to tend bar along with his daughter Margaret. A Michigan law allowed the wives or daughters of a licensed bar owner to work as bartenders but prohibited the hiring of other women. When a male applicant for a bartender's job was turned down by Goesart, he filed suit for enforcement of the law banning women bartenders.

Davidow thought she had a good case that would help women achieve equal employment opportunities. Since the oft-stated reason for the law was that women bartenders were in danger of having their morals corrupted, Davidow pointed out that Michigan women were permitted to be barmaids, serving drinks on the floor of the establishment, but not allowed to serve or make drinks behind the bar. Yet surely out in the open bar or restaurant, she reasoned, barmaids were much more likely to be harassed by customers than behind the protective cover of the bar itself.

When *Goesart* v. *Cleary* was heard by the Supreme Court in 1948, Davidow lost her case. It apparently did not matter that women had worked in every conceivable occupation during the war. The majority opinion declared that "the Constitution does not require legislatures to reflect . . . shifting social standards."[6] Women would continue to be legally typecast into "female" occupations for the next sixteen years.

Under different circumstances, a new movement for women's equality might have emerged in the postwar period. But larger forces were at work that would effectively gag the precious right to free speech for the next fifteen years.

Mary Kaufman, the labor lawyer from New York (see Chapter 4), became aware of the change soon after the end of the war. As Europe's concentration camps like Auschwitz and Bergen-Belsen were liberated by Allied troops, the murders of 6 million Jews by the Nazis became common knowledge. Under enormous pressure to punish the mass murderers, the Allies held trials in Nuremburg, Germany, to prosecute top Nazi war criminals.

Two Jewish women lawyers, Kaufman and Cecelia Goetz, fought for and obtained jobs on the Allies' prosecution team. When Goetz was hired, she was required to sign a waiver of disability. Her "disability" was her female condition!

In Nuremburg, Kaufman was assigned to the team prosecuting the board of directors of the I. G. Farben Company, a major producer of armaments for the Nazis with connections in dozens of countries. A group of convicted saboteurs, trained by I. G. Farben, had been caught in the United States and convicted during the war. They had been sent back after the war to continue serving their sentences in Germany. Kaufman subpoenaed them to testify.[7]

Kaufman later recalled with bitterness that before she could call them to the witness stand, a superior ordered her to cancel the subpoenas and send the witnesses back to their cells "because the State Department was kicking up quite a fuss. That closed the door to proof of Farben's role in the sabotage effort."

Without the key testimony, I. G. Farben was found not guilty. "I'll never forget the day when we sat and listened to the Tribunal's opinion and judgment," Kaufman sadly recalled. "We were terribly depressed. . . . We knew that the decision was politically motivated."[8]

But it was not until long after she returned home, in 1948, that Kaufman understood why the State Department had shielded I. G. Farben's board.

The friendship between the United States and the Soviet Union, wartime Allies in the struggle against the Axis powers, had crumbled. The Soviet Union had been labeled as the new enemy. There were many reasons for the sudden turnabout.

An ideological battle was taking shape throughout much of the world. Nations like France, governed during the war years by Nazi occupiers and collaborators, and Italy, where the fascist dictator Benito Mussolini had held power for decades, were about to elect new governments. In far-flung colonies in Asia and Africa, people newly liberated from German and Japanese control were demanding independence from their colonial rulers. In China a popular revolution was placing the communist Mao Tse Tung in power. The Soviet Union and the United States were both attempting to influence the choices between socialism or capitalism that would determine the control of future world markets. Some scholars also maintain that American policy makers, in order to stop the U.S. economy from backsliding into a revived Depression once war industries shut down, needed to create a new enemy, the "Red Menace," as the reason for keeping the armaments industry producing.

But not all Americans accepted the idea that the Soviet Union was a genuine world threat. Nazi armies had invaded the Soviet Union, leaving its economy in ruins and millions dead. Many Soviet and American citizens were urging a policy of peaceful coexistence between the two largest world powers. Their voices were quickly silenced by a national anticommunist hysteria called the "witch-hunt" and "McCarthyism," after Senator Joseph McCarthy of Wisconsin.

The U.S. attorney general produced a list of dozens of "subversive" organizations. Although the list included the Communist Party, it also included most groups that had fought for equality, workers' rights, and immigrant rights; and organizations as disparate as environmental groups like Nature Friends of America and even the Chopin Cultural Center. People who had even briefly belonged to any of these organizations or supported issues like world peace, a ban on nuclear tests, and even equal rights for minorities were in danger of being labeled "un-American" and losing their jobs.

Over the next fifteen years, fear induced by this modern witch-hunt inhibited free speech in the United States. Thousands were fired from their jobs—teachers, filmmakers, factory and restaurant workers. President Harry S. Truman issued Executive Order 9835, assigning a special board of Civil Service commissioners to check on government employees and fire anyone who had been shown to be a sympathizer of a listed suspect organization. Those accused had no right to a hearing or even to face their accusers. Because women lawyers had been prominent in labor law, civil liberties law, and poverty law, they became especially vulnerable targets for the witch-hunters. Dorothy Kenyon, for example, New York City's first woman deputy commissioner of licenses and a well-known fighter for civil liberties, was named by McCarthy during his attacks on suspected communists in government. Kenyon called him "an unmitigated liar, a coward to take shelter in the cloak of congressional immunity."[9]

Most people did not fight back to stop the witch-hunt and demand respect for the Bill of Rights. The Cold War had indeed succeeded in keeping the economy in high gear. Americans bought homes, appliances, and cars. But in the spring of 1954, McCarthy went one step too far when he held hearings on "subversives" in the military. The Army went on the offensive against McCarthy, and several months later the Senate voted to censure him. Although Senator McCarthy was out of favor, the Cold War was alive and well.

A few women lawyers were among a tiny group of Americans who continued to openly oppose Cold War policies. Mary Kaufman was among them. She realized that leaders of the German company I. G. Farben, as well as other notorious Nazis, had been shielded from prosecution as war criminals by the U.S. State Department. These Nazis could provide valuable information to the Central Intelligence Agency (CIA) on the Communists who had been among the valiant anti-Nazi resistance fighters of Europe. This dismaying truth was not fully revealed to the public until many years later. It was now apparent that in the heyday of the Cold War, the U.S. government had decided that a few prominent Nazi leaders would be valuable assets in the fight against communism in general. (In *The World at Arms,* Reader's Digest Illustrated History of World War II, p. 450, the U.S. role is discussed.)

The case of Klaus Barbie, the Gestapo chief in German-occupied France during World War II, is a notorious example of that U.S. policy. Barbie became known as "the Butcher of Lyons" because he had ordered the deportation of thousands of French resistance fighters and Jews to Hitler's death camps. After the war, the CIA and U.S. military intelligence secretly brought Barbie to the United States to help them compile lists of Europe's Resistance activists as part of their anticommunist campaign. In 1951 Barbie was smuggled into Bolivia with a new identity, where he lived a life of luxury helping Bolivia's military regime suppress opposition. The truth came out in 1983, when Nazi hunters found Barbie in South America and returned him to France, where he was tried and convicted as a mass murderer.[10]

The atmosphere of fear was so great during the witch-hunt phase of the Cold War that, as one researcher put it, "The rights lawyers in the ACLU fell over each other in the rush to proclaim their patriotism. They were not willing, either in court or in front of congressional committees, to defend the victims of what is commonly called McCarthyism."[11] Kaufman joined the ranks of a few brave attorneys who dared to test Cold War legislation in the courts. She became part of the legal team that defended people who were being prosecuted under a law called Smith Act.

This act was being used to silence left-wing political parties. Leaders of the Socialist Workers Party, despite their critical attitude toward Soviet-style undemocratic socialism, were tried, convicted, and sent off to jail in 1943 for the simple act of advocating and teaching socialism. In 1949, twelve leaders of the American Communist Party were indicted. A nine-month trial followed, during which Kaufman was part of the defense team. But despite her trial experience, Kaufman was kept behind a desk while the male attorneys went to the courtroom.

When the trial was over, not only were the Smith Act defendants jailed but the trial judge, Harold Medina, charged their lawyers with contempt and sentenced them to prison terms. Kaufman, of course, kept her freedom because she had not been involved in the courtroom work. Later she described her feelings:

> As I sat there all alone at counsel table while the others stood, I was again profoundly ashamed of my country. The atmosphere of fear already had its firm grip on the American people. The trial lawyers in that case had performed brilliantly and courageously. But I'm ashamed to say they did not get the support of most of the members of the bar. All of the lawyers served time in jail . . . and were hounded in a variety of ways, including disbarment. But . . . [they] were eventually vindicated and reinstated to the bar.[12]

Just as Caroline Lowe had defended IWW leaders in 1917, Kaufman traveled all over the country defending other people indicted under the Smith Act. Often she depended entirely on money raised by defense committees to help house and feed herself and her son. She continued with this work until a Supreme Court decision in 1957 watered down the Smith Act. Then she went into private practice. It was another war, in far-away Vietnam, that brought her back into the fray less than ten years later.

During the first decade of the Cold War, even the idea of government guarantees of legal rights for the poor could be labeled "un-American." In Great Britain, a 1950 law required every member of the bar to be available to represent clients who were unable to pay for their own defense.[13] In the United States, the National Lawyers Guild pressed for the same type of law, pointing out that two-thirds of all defendants could not pay for legal services. In response, the ABA launched a widespread campaign against such a law, labeling the British law as "Socialist." The ABA's Special Committee to Study Communist Tactics, Strategy and Objectives even recommended that guild members be forced to take loyalty oaths or be disbarred.

Some members of the legal profession took a less extreme position. They simply did not want to be obligated by law to donate a few precious "billable hours" to poor defendants at lower fees. Instead they supported the expansion of Legal Aid services. By 1960, although more Legal Aid offices had been opened, there was still a great need.

Surprisingly, the competition between the Soviet Union and Eastern Europe on the one hand and the United States and Western Europe on the other produced some unintended benefits for racial minorities and women in the United States. The Soviet press filled its pages regularly with stories about racism against African Americans in the United States. Occasionally the subordinate role of women was also described. Soviet journalists boasted that in the socialist Soviet Union women had equal access to education and the professions, while in the United States, by 1950, women earned only one-fourth of all bachelor's degrees, their lowest share since the 1920s. Placement in colleges had become more difficult as World War II veterans took advantage of a government program called the GI Bill and returned to school.[14] As more colleges opened, the situation was quickly rectified.

It is not unlikely that Cold War pressures had something to do with Harvard Law School's Dean Irwin Griswold's announcement in the fall of 1949 that Harvard Law School would accept "a small number of unusually qualified women students."

The twelve women of the first coed class of 1950 received a less than friendly welcome. Griswold greeted them with the words, "I didn't favor your admission, but since you are here, welcome."

The male students were no friendlier. In the Harvard student newspaper, a poem appeared in response to the presence of women on campus:

We'll mourn the harried profs' morale,
As classes just are not the same,
FOR NO ONE QUESTIONS LIKE A GAL,
And no one reasons like a dame,
Two years of staring at these walls,
(With sour judges pictured there)
Of trudging through depressing halls,
Of reading law, dull legal books,
Have made me sigh for long blonde curls,
For sweet young things with lots of looks;
And so I say "Bring on the girls!"

Ladies' Day at the law school was particularly humiliating for the women students. They were required to

126

present cases for the entertainment of the class and then undergo a grilling by their professors. Some professors assigned only lurid sex crime cases to the women. Charlotte Horwood Armstrong later recalled how one professor, whose "style was teaching by humiliation . . . took sadistic delight in hounding women."[15]

Congresswoman Patricia Schroeder of Colorado, who entered Harvard Law School in 1961, recounted similar unpleasant experiences:

> The women in the law school were treated like Amazons. Men wanted cute blondes from Lesley [a junior college near Harvard]. Among the men there was a feeling that Harvard Law School had been ruined because they let girls in.[16]

Women law students put up with these difficulties because they believed that an Ivy League degree would help them find better jobs. But they quickly discovered that most law firms refused to even interview them. Out of 1,755 women attorneys in New York in 1957, only eighteen worked for large firms.

It is no less than amazing that any women continued to study for law careers. Ruth Bader Ginsburg, for example, appointed as associate justice of the U.S. Supreme Court by President Bill Clinton in 1994, was one of nine women in a class of 500 entering Harvard in 1956. Attributing the small numbers of women law students to both resistance by universities and fewer female applicants, Ginsburg explained it this way:

> Why were there so few women in law school a generation ago? It was the sense that, well, I can go through three years of law school and then what? Who will hire me and how will I support myself? . . . So many places were closed to women in those days. The most prestigious

Ruth Bader Ginsburg, the second woman to sit on the
Supreme Court, was one of only nine women in an entering
class of 500 in Harvard Law school in 1956.

clerkships with judges were not open to women. Some of our most distinguished jurists simply refused to interview a female.[17]

At the end of her second year, when her husband was offered a job in New York City, Ginsburg transferred to Columbia Law School, graduating in 1959. Although she tied for first place in her class, not one law firm was interested in hiring her. Through the route that many women law graduates used in those days—connections—she landed a job clerking for a federal district court judge. Later she worked on a research project on international law at Columbia and then landed a teaching post at Rutgers University in 1963, an unusual job for a woman lawyer.

Sandra Day O'Connor, the first woman appointed to the Supreme Court in 1981, was third highest in her class when she graduated from Stanford Law School in 1951. She managed to interview with a few law firms but "none had ever hired a woman before as a lawyer, and they were not prepared to do so."[18] The only job offer she received was as a legal secretary in Los Angeles. O'Connor turned to part-time legal work, volunteer work, and raising a family, not returning to full-time employment until 1965.[19]

Like both of these exceptionally talented women, most women lawyers in the 1950s faced the same limited choices as their predecessors. The government hired a few more women attorneys, and most of them turned in outstanding performances.

Ida Klaus, for example, one of the first women law graduates of Columbia University, was hired by the National Labor Relations Board in 1948. In 1954, New York City mayor Robert F. Wagner appointed her as counsel to his new Department of Labor. Klaus wrote the famous "Little Wagner Act," expanding the right to collective bargaining. In 1961 she was appointed as

Sandra Day O'Conner, the first female
Supreme Court justice, couldn't get a job as a lawyer
when she graduated from law school.

chief adviser to John F. Kennedy's task force on collective bargaining among federal employees. From 1962 until her retirement in 1975, she was the chief labor negotiator for New York City's Board of Education and director of staff relations.

The long-standing opposition to women as criminal lawyers remained firmly in place. Ruth Bader Ginsburg described it this way:

> No U.S. Attorney's office would hire a woman as a prosecutor. U.S. attorneys were beginning to hire women for civil litigation, but not for criminal cases. That seemed to me ironic. The excuse was women are too soft, they can't handle hardened criminal types. But if you looked at the other side of the street to see who was defending indigent defendants, it was Legal Aid. Legal Aid was full of women. The relationship between the defendant and the defense lawyer is much closer than that between the prosecutor and the accused. So it wasn't women's inability to deal with hardened criminals. Women did just that in Legal Aid.

Chicago attorney Carole K. Bellows was a law student at Northwestern University in the 1950s when a member of the Chicago Bar came to the school to encourage students to become criminal lawyers. Four women were seated among almost 100 men. Before he started his talk, he announced, "I'm here to recruit investigators for the committee which represents indigent defendants in criminal cases. It is not necessary for any women to stay here. We can't use them."[20]

Even in the 1960s, college women were discouraged from pursuing "masculine" studies like mathematics, the sciences, engineering, and medicine and law. Elementary school teaching, nursing, and nutritional fields

131

remained the "feminine" majors. Amazingly, in 1962, when a new women's college, Winthrop, opened in South Carolina, its catalog was strikingly similar to those of the pre–Civil War female seminaries. Courses designed for "young ladies" emphasized "stenography, typewriting . . . designing . . . needlework, cooking, housekeeping and such other industrial arts as may be suitable to their sex and conducive to their support and usefulness."[21]

"We had no idea that we were part of an inherited social contract that required our inequality," lawyer Mona Harrington wrote in 1994.[22] Even for the few activists who were angry over sex discrimination, racism was the issue most on their minds, just as the horrors of slavery had overshadowed the problems of women's inequality in the Civil War era.

The government experts apparently agreed. Racial segregation and discrimination was the most obvious contradiction to America's desire for a world image of genuine democracy and equality. In 1954 the unanimous U.S. Supreme Court school desegregation decision in *Brown* v. *The Board of Education* negated the separate-but-equal provision that it had upheld in the 1890s.

Yet despite this landmark decision on racial equality, over the next decade when the Court heard cases for women's equality, its rulings were almost always unfavorable. On the issue of women serving as jurors, for example, a negative Supreme Court ruling in 1960 perplexed many who had cheered the *Brown* decision.[23] When an all-male Florida jury found Evangeline Hoyt guilty of murdering her husband, her lawyers had appealed the verdict all the way to the Supreme Court on the basis that Hoyt had been deprived of her equal protection rights to a trial by a jury of her peers. Many Court watchers were sure that the Supreme Court would rule in favor of Hoyt. In

1935, after all, the Court had ruled that African Americans could not receive a fair trial where blacks were excluded from juries.

But the justices saw no parallel between all male juries at women's trials and all-white juries at the trials of African Americans. Like a strange echo of Justice Bradley's decision in the case of Myra Bradwell almost a century earlier, Chief Justice Warren Burger called Florida's jury selection law "a reasonable accommodation of women's role as the center of home and family life," adding, "This case in no way resembles those involving race or color." The Supreme Court thereby affirmed the rights of states to exempt all women from jury duty, from age twenty-one to 100, married or single, with or without small children.

With this mood prevailing even in the highest court, there was little chance of introducing new legislation on women's legal rights, even on a state-by-state basis. Forty years after women had won the right to vote, women in decision-making positions—whether in Congress or state legislatures—remained "rare birds." Women on the bench were just as scarce.

Influential women had been pressuring the administration to appoint a woman to the Supreme Court. Florence Ellinwood Allen, justice of the Sixth Circuit Court of Appeals since 1934, was often suggested as a possible candidate. President Truman informed her supporters that he had talked the possibility over with the Supreme Court justices and they had opposed such a move. Perhaps to soften his critics, as well as to win points in the Cold War, he nominated Burnita Shelton Matthews, an ardent feminist, to a judgeship in a federal district court in 1949. In 1919, Matthews had been among the women picketing the White House for the right to vote and had written extensively on the legal rights of her sex.

Whenever a strong push was made for the promotion of women, one or two token women received prestigious appointments. In the early sixties, pressure from Puerto Rican leaders led to the hiring of Irma Vidal Santaella, the first Puerto Rican woman lawyer in New York State, as an adviser to two senators, Robert F. Kennedy and Jacob Javits, on the issue of voting rights for Puerto Ricans.[24] In 1960, Lorna E. Lockwood became the first woman member of a state supreme court when she was elected to the Arizona Supreme Court, later becoming the chief justice.

A few black women continued to graduate from law schools each year, but their job-hunting prospects showed little improvement. A white woman attorney, Marian Sullivan, came to realize how difficult things were for black women during her own discouraging search for work in the 1950s.

> I remember one day when I was feeling particularly awful, a receptionist called me over to deliver still one more rejection. She thought she would make me feel better by telling me how they had just rejected a colored girl who had the *nerve* to apply for the position. I remember thinking no matter how bad it was for me, it had to be worse for her. I never learned who she was but that night I went home and said a prayer for her.[25]

Despite these difficulties, some young black women decided to study law specifically to attempt to win equality for African Americans, long before Dr. Martin Luther King, Jr.'s "I Have a Dream Speech" in 1963. They were moved by the struggles of black men during World War II for the right to fight for their country. African American servicemen were almost always assigned to segregated all-black service units commanded by white officers, usually so-called service units for burial duty, garbage duty, and driving the trucks over roads peppered with dangerous land mines to deliver military goods to the front. In the Navy they were permitted to serve only as messmen, performing kitchen duties in the holds of the ships. The symbol of the civil rights movement during that period was a double *V*: *V* for victory against the Axis Powers and *V* for victory against racism at home.

When black veterans came home, the very sight of them in uniform enraged segregationists of the South as well as prejudiced people throughout the land.[26] Black veterans were physically attacked. The case that moved President Truman to take action on civil rights was the attack on Sergeant Isaac Woodard, Jr., in February 1946. Pulled off a bus by police in South Carolina, he was savagely beaten and blinded by nightsticks poked into his eyes.

A powerful alliance emerged at the end of the war between Jewish Americans, African Americans, and other groups. All over the nation, interracial and interfaith conferences were held. Court cases often became joint enterprises to attempt to reverse segregation in public places.[27]

Under pressure to act to ensure civil rights, President Truman, afraid of offending his Democratic Party supporters in the South, stalled. When he finally agreed to meet with a delegation of black civil rights and human rights leaders, he heard about the shocking crime against Woodard and reportedly said, "We've got to do something!"[28]

President Truman soon issued Executive Order 9808, creating the President's Committee on Civil Rights (PCCR) and instructing its members to make recommendations on civil rights. Sadie Alexander, one of the handful of pioneer black women attorneys (see Chapter 4), was a member of the PCCR and coauthored its report, *To Secure These Rights.* Raising the fact that Soviet leaders "have tried to prove our democracy an empty fraud, and our nation a consistent oppressor of underprivileged people,"[29] the document called for comprehensive civil rights legislation.

Recommendations were one thing. Moving Congress was another. Truman pressed forward on the issue of military integration, and a few blacks were moved into public prominence. Jackie Robinson was hired by the Brooklyn Dodgers in 1946 and became the first black baseball player on a modern major league team in 1947—the first and *last* for several more years.

Although Robinson's appearance on baseball diamonds produced brief euphoria, black Americans were also concerned over housing and job discrimination in their everyday life. Tempers flared when a new military draft law was proposed on the floor of Congress in 1947, with continued segregation included in it.

At the Democratic National Convention, liberal delegates pushed through a stronger than usual section on civil rights in the party's platform, causing a number of southern delegates to storm out and go home to form a new States' Rights Party. No longer pinned into inaction by the South, Truman moved to win the support of civil rights advocates by cautiously starting the ball rolling on military integration. He issued Executive Order 9981, calling for equality of opportunity for all persons in the armed services, without specifically mentioning integration.

Truman won the election, receiving 60 percent of the black vote. Hopes rose that the president would now push ahead on civil rights, but despite a few appointments of African Americans to judgeships and other government posts, and very slow progress toward military integration, discrimination in all its ugly forms remained intact.

A number of black women attorneys achieved prominence during these early struggles. Ruth Harvey Charity, who grew up in Virginia, remembered feeling anger over segregation from her earliest childhood.

Constance Baker Motley, a lawyer for the NAACP
during the civil rights period, became the first black woman
to be elected Manhattan Borough President in 1965.
New York Mayor Robert Wagner is swearing her in.

Deciding to study law, Charity attended Howard University. Even at Howard she was confronted with the sexism of black men, when they asked her why she had not majored in home economics.[30]

In 1944, Charity helped to organize the first victorious sit-in at a Washington, D.C., restaurant. After she graduated, Charity went into private practice back in her hometown. She instituted suits against the city demanding desegregation of the library and the city park, and proving that the facilities for blacks were indeed separate but totally unequal. The case she considered her most important though was her defense and the subsequent acquittal of more than a thousand civil rights demonstrators arrested in Danville, Virginia, in 1963.

But the rights of black women, even when they were violated by black men, were another important cause for Charity. In the organization for black attorneys, the National Bar Association, women lawyers were always given secretarial assignments. Charity and another black woman attorney organized a women's division of the NBA and later formed the National Association of Black Women Attorneys. As so many successful women lawyers did, Charity assisted other women in their efforts to enter the legal profession. "After all, if we don't bring them along, who will?" she once remarked.[31]

The best-known African American woman lawyer of that period was Constance Baker Motley. Motley was on the NAACP legal team that achieved the Supreme Court 1954 school desegregation decision. She was also one of the very few black attorneys to come from a poor family.[32]

In 1938 Motley attended a meeting at her high school and heard an attorney discuss a recent NAACP separate-but-equal case. Motley started dreaming about a law career but realized that she had no money for her schooling. Two years later when the same speaker appeared at the local Community House, Motley was there. Clarence W. Blakeslee, a wealthy white Connecticut businessman, had donated the money for the center and asked those gathered at the meeting why so few black people used the facility. Young Motley took the floor and told him that the people who ran the Community House did not understand the needs of the black people of the area.

Impressed by the outspoken young woman, Blakeslee decided to foot the bill for her education. Constance Motley entered all-black Fisk University in Nashville in 1941 but was shaken by southern segregation. Excluded from theaters and restaurants and even unable to try on clothes in department stores, Motley transferred to New York University and then went on to Columbia Law School, the second black woman ever accepted there.

After graduation, Motley was hired by Thurgood Marshall, the director of the NAACP Legal Defense Fund and later the first black Supreme Court justice. She went to work arguing segregation cases, many of them in the South. In southern courtrooms, black men and women were never addressed as "Mr." or "Mrs." Judges persisted in calling Motley "Connie." Barred from local hotels, she had to find housing with NAACP supporters in the area. Constance Baker Motley was a dynamo in court, arguing ten cases before the Supreme Court and losing only one of them. During the height of the civil rights struggle in the 1960s, she served as one of Dr. Martin Luther King, Jr.'s lawyers in Birmingham, Alabama.

A few black women pioneer lawyers were appointed to posts in city governments. Jane M. Bolin, the first black woman judge in New York, was appointed by New York's mayor LaGuardia in 1939 for a ten-year term, and was reappointed by every subsequent mayor until her retirement in 1979. President Truman selected a few pioneer black women attorneys, Eunice Carter among them, for visible posts, especially in the United Nations. Marjorie McKenzie Lawson was active in John F. Kennedy's election campaign of 1960, advising party leaders on civil rights issues and later winning a juvenile court judgeship. Lyndon Baines Johnson appointed her as United States representative to the Social Commission of the United Nations Economic and Social Council.

Edith Sampson was appointed as an alternate U.S. representative to the United Nations General Assembly in 1950 and was sent on tours to speak on the status of blacks in the United States, a very touchy Cold War issue. Several black journalists accused her of playing down racial issues in order to support the government's anti-Communist propaganda. Sampson herself admitted, "There were times when I had to bow my head in shame when talking about how some Negroes have been treated in the United States."[33] In 1962, Sampson was elected associate judge of the Municipal Court of Chicago, the first black woman so elected in the United States. But both black women and white women lawyers remained in the backwaters of the profession until civil rights legislation, the result of the Civil Rights Movement, had a profound impact on *all* of them, to the surprise of many.

Perhaps if the southern segregationists had remained calm, civil rights and equal rights for women would have been delayed for another twenty or thirty years. The Supreme Court had set no timetable for school integration beyond a vague order in 1955 that it should be accomplished with "all deliberate speed."[34] But segregationists throughout the South panicked and rushed to take preventive action. The Ku Klux Klan and newly formed White Citizens Councils recruited thousands of people to make sure integration would *never* come to pass.

140

Almost ten years of violence lay ahead, during which television viewers all over the nation would become fully aware of the events in the South. In the summer of 1955, the nation learned about the murder of a fourteen-year-old black teenager from Chicago, Emmett Till. Kidnapped from his grandfather's house in Mississippi and murdered for the "crime" of allegedly flirting with a white girl, Till's mutilated body was thrown into the Tallahachie River. An all-white, all-male jury found his killers not guilty.

On December 1, 1955, in Montgomery, Alabama, a tired black seamstress named Rosa Parks, who was also secretary of the local NAACP, boarded a bus after a hard day's work and took the last remaining empty seat in the first row of the "colored" section. When a white man came on board, the driver ordered Mrs. Parks to give him her seat. When she refused, he called the police and Parks was arrested.

Within days the Montgomery Bus Boycott was launched, led by a young minister named Dr. Martin Luther King, Jr. For almost a year the 42,000 African American working people in Montgomery refused to ride the segregated buses, instead walking and arranging car pools to get to their jobs. Some white employers risked public criticism by transporting their own much needed maids and baby-sitters. Despite the arrest and harassment of black leaders and even the bombing of four black churches, the movement could not be stopped. A year later the buses were integrated.

Television news showed poignant footage in the fall of 1957 of one small, lone fifteen-year-old black girl, Elizabeth Eckford, attempting to attend classes in a high school in Little Rock, Arkansas. A mob of screaming men and women lined the path to the school entrance, cursing and spitting at her. Many Americans were shocked. Eckford's tormenters were not Ku Klux Klanners in white sheets or terrorists speeding in the night with their bombs, but ordinary-looking mothers, fathers, grandmothers.

Later, viewers watched as Mississippi governor Ross Barnett blocked the door of the administration building at the University of Mississippi to prevent a black man, James Meredith, from registering. Thousands of students and adults waved Confederate flags. They threw gas bombs and bricks at federal marshals and reporters for fifteen hours. President Kennedy ordered in 12,000 troops. When the rioting ended, 400 people had been injured and two were dead.

Americans of every race and religion began to react to the disgraceful events. Angry letters and phone calls demanding firm federal action poured into the White House.

Now the Civil Rights Movement could not be stopped by government-enforced token school integration. On February 1, 1960, in Greensboro, North Carolina, four black students occupied stools at the local Woolworth's lunch counter. Refused service, they stayed until the store closed. In some northern cities, black and white youths and adults began picketing local Woolworth's, demanding that the company change its policies in the South. Some jumped on buses and headed South to put their own bodies on the line. They were arrested and sang the new anthem of the movement, "We Shall Overcome," in their jail cells.

In the next twelve months, more than 50,000 young people—most black, some white—participated in sit-ins in a hundred southern cities. Over 3,600 were jailed. Faced with serious losses of income, many southern businessmen integrated their lunch counters.

With the conflict over black civil rights capturing the attention of the nation, in 1961, few noticed the news that President John F. Kennedy through an executive order had appointed a President's Commission on the Status of Women. The commission was asked to explore "additional affirmative steps which should be taken through legislation, executive or administrative action to assure non-discrimination on the basis of sex and to enhance constructive employment opportunities for women." Kennedy told the press, "I see thousands of women getting out of colleges each year. . . . What chance do they have to make full use of their powers?"[35]

It was the first time that the issue of women's equality was made part of the federal government's agenda. But the public was used to the setting up of commissions, committees, and government-funded studies to look into long-standing problems. Often there were few results from such projects.

Although many women with college degrees were sitting at home in the suburbs, with their career aspirations set aside, by 1958, 43 percent of all women were in the workforce, many of them helping to support their families, and some of them the only source of their family income. Betty Friedan's book, *The Feminine Mystique,* became an overnight best-seller in 1963. In it she addressed the dilemma of women staying home in the suburbs, suffering from "the problem that had no name," a sense of worthlessness and boredom. She expressed ideas that many of them had secretly held. They had the right to have careers and raise children, she told them, the right to walk away from the happy homemaker image and make their own life decisions.

Undoubtedly at least some of the members of President Kennedy's commission, many of them mothers and career women, were moved by Friedan's work. The commission's Committee on Private Employment recommended legislation for equal pay for women that would "place main reliance on persuasion and voluntary compliance."[36] The Federal Equal Pay Act was passed in 1963 as an amendment to the Fair Labor Standards Act.[37] The new law made it possible for women to sue to win equal pay in their jobs as well as to gain back pay if they had been previously cheated. The problem with the legislation was that most women worked at so-called female jobs, not comparable to those held by men. When they worked at the same jobs, their titles were often different. Female bank clerks, for example, were called tellers, while men doing the same work were called management trainees. Only a few women had the time or financial resources to take their cases to court, and voluntary compliance was a rare event.

The news of black and white students' riding on buses together through the South in "Freedom Rides" created far more excitement. The Supreme Court had ruled that segregation was illegal in interstate bus travel, which included bus terminal restaurants and waiting rooms. Although the Freedom Riders were upholding the law of the land, the federal government offered them no protection. Their buses were set on fire by southern mobs, and many were severely beaten and jailed while FBI agents observed.

As the situation worsened, people from all over the nation flocked to join the courageous demonstrators, not only students but ministers, teachers, and housewives. In June 1962, civil rights leader Medgar Evers was killed by an assassin's bullet in his back in the driveway of his home in Jackson, Mississippi, and still the movement grew.

In the spring of 1963, many Americans watched their television screens in horror as police and firemen in Birmingham, Alabama, turned high-power hoses, tear gas, and trained attack dogs on civil rights marchers. As people were savagely beaten and bitten and ambulances screamed onto the scene, the demonstrators chanted: "The whole world is watching."

And so it was. Inundated with letters, phone calls, and telegrams, President Kennedy sent a government team to negotiate. Birmingham businessmen agreed to allow blacks to eat at their lunch counters. But with each modest victory, the violence escalated. A bomb exploded at the motel where Martin Luther King, Jr., and other leaders were staying.

On August 28, 1963, a quarter of a million Americans streamed into the capital and marched to the Lincoln Memorial to join the March on Washington for Jobs and Freedom, where they heard Dr. King's stirring "I Have a Dream" speech. Eighteen days later, four little black girls attending Sunday school in the basement of Birmingham's Sixteenth Street Church were blown to bits when a bomb exploded.

On November 22, 1963, President John F. Kennedy was assassinated in Dallas, Texas, and Lyndon B. Johnson was inaugurated as president. It was obvious to the new president that the Civil Rights Movement was not about to disappear.

The first comprehensive civil rights act since Reconstruction was introduced in Congress.[38] One of its most hotly contested sections, Title VII, prohibited employment discrimination on the basis of race, color, religion, or national origin. A proposal in the House Rules Committee to add the word *sex*, making job discrimination against women illegal as well, was defeated, 8 to 7. Oregon's representative Edith Green later claimed that any legislation for equal opportunity in hiring and promotion of women "considered by itself . . . would not have received 100 votes."[39]

A group of southern Democrats and conservative states' rights Republicans used the sex discrimination issue to try to prevent passage of the civil rights legislation. Howard W. Smith, an eighty-one-year-old congressman from Virginia, offered an amendment to Title VII of the Civil Rights Act including sex along with race, color, and national origin.

At first it appeared that Smith's tactic would work. Laughter burst out on the floor of Congress when Smith argued that his amendment would "protect our spinster friends in their 'right' to a husband and family." Even a usually liberal congressman, like Emanuel Celler, defeated in 1972 by Elizabeth Holtzman, a woman lawyer, threw in his little joke: "I usually have the last two words, and those words are 'Yes, dear.'"[40]

Some strong supporters of the Civil Rights Act tried to defeat the amendment "before it sank the bill under gales of laughter." Representative Edith Green—who feared that Smith's amendment would be used to defeat Title VII, as Smith intended—was among them.

While the violence in the South continued, the debate on the Civil Rights Act dragged on for four months. Congresswoman Martha Griffiths decided that it was time to act, even if it meant playing up to the racism of some of her colleagues. Griffiths rose to speak while "the room was rocking with laughter" and angrily addressed the assembled congressmen.

> If there were any need to prove your disrespect you've already proved it by your laughter. We've sat here for four days discussing the rights of blacks and other minorities and there has been no laughter, not even a smile. But when we suggest that you shouldn't discriminate against your own wives, your own mothers, your own granddaughters, your own sisters, then you laugh.

The room fell silent as Congresswoman Griffiths continued:

> You have succeeded in dividing American labor into three parts. First are American white men, who stand at the top and will get what they've always gotten. Then you're going to put in black men and women. And the third class will be your mothers, your wives, your widows, your daughters

and your sisters. They will be the last hired and the first fired. Why are you doing this? Add sex. Why discriminate against white women?[41]

Two days later, the House of Representatives passed the Civil Rights Act with the prohibition of sex discrimination included and sent it on to the Senate. Howard W. Smith stated for the benefit of his segregationist supporters in Virginia, "I have certainly tried to do everything I could to hinder, delay and dilapidate this bill."

The issue of women's equality was barely mentioned in the press, although a *New York Times* editorial commented that "the civil rights forces had to accept some unexpected amendments." The *Times* reduced the entire victory to a joke, declaring, "Better if Congress had just abolished sex itself. A maid can now be a man. Girl Friday is an intolerable offense. . . . Boy wanted—has reached its last chapter."[42]

Civil rights leaders, knowing that the Senate would be an even greater stumbling block to passage of the urgent legislation, decided that it was time to coordinate their efforts and intensify the struggle. A massive voter registration drive was organized in Mississippi, with all of the civil rights groups cooperating. By the early summer of 1964, some 1,200 people arrived in Mississippi.

Among them was Anna Diggs Taylor, a young black attorney who volunteered to work without pay with the seventy lawyers sent by the National Lawyers Guild to handle the hundreds of arrests and subsequent civil rights cases expected during "Mississippi Freedom Summer." Taylor had attended Yale Law School on a scholarship and earned her law degree. She had been an assistant prosecutor in Detroit since 1961. But the events in the South mattered more to her than her own career aspirations. Like the other volunteers for Mississippi

147

Freedom Summer, she certainly expected trouble, but perhaps not the horrors that were about to unfold.

Twenty-five-year-old Michael "Mickey" Schwerner and his wife Rita, both New Yorkers, were among the volunteers to the Freedom Summer Project organized by the Student Nonviolent Coordinating Committee (SNCC). They were already in Mississippi, running a community center in the small town of Meridian, offering story hours for children and courses in African American history. Working with them was James Earl Chaney, a young black man from the area. When the school term ended, Andrew Goodman, a twenty-year-old student from New York City, joined them.

The debate over the Civil Rights Act had stalled in the Senate. For seventy-five days southern congressmen conducted a filibuster to block a vote. On June 10, 1964, the Senate voted 71 to 29 for cloture—the cutting off of debate and an immediate vote. On June 19 the Senate approved the Civil Rights Act of 1964, by a vote of 73 to 27. It returned the bill to the House for what was certain to be final approval.

Southern racists responded with an instantaneous escalation of their violence. The following day, as Schwerner, Chaney, and Goodman drove to the nearby town of Longdale, where a black church had been burned down to the ground, they must have heard the heartening news of the Senate vote on their car radio. They never returned to Meridian. When it was learned that the three men had disappeared, police in nearby Philadelphia, Mississippi, said they had taken them to jail for speeding and then released them. President Johnson sent in 200 FBI agents to investigate the disappearance. Attention around the world was focused for many weeks on the missing civil rights workers.

On July 2, while the search for the three civil rights workers continued, the House of Representatives voted

148

289 to 126 for final passage of the Civil Rights Act. Five hours later, President Johnson signed the bill into law. On August 4, 1964, the bodies of Chaney, Goodman, and Schwerner were found buried deep in an earthen dam.

Students coming back from the South after participating in Freedom Summer of 1964 were not willing to return to normal everyday activities. At the University of California campus in Berkeley, a few set up tables with SNCC literature. When campus officials ordered them to stop, they refused and the Free Speech Movement (FSM) was born. Soon, college students throughout the nation were organizing for free speech rights, civil rights, and an end to an escalating, unpopular war in Vietnam.

Most of the elected officials in the South continued to defy the Civil Rights Act. As racist violence continued, the Civil Rights Movement grew even larger. When SNCC leader John Lewis was clubbed down leading a protest march in Selma, Alabama, 25,000 people, including many prominent religious leaders and celebrities, answered Dr. King's call for a larger demonstration. Four months later, the Voting Rights Act of 1965 declared voter registration tests illegal.

The inclusion of women in the Civil Rights Act of 1964 was all but forgotten. Sex discrimination by employers, employment agencies, and even unions did not suddenly end. Few violators were willing to comply with the new law unless court orders forced them to do so. The government set up the Equal Employment Opportunities Commission (EEOC), headed by Franklin Delano Roosevelt, Jr., to enforce the Civil Rights Act, but it was clear that the issue of sex discrimination was not on the EEOC's priority list. Herman Edelsberg, executive director, informed the press that he thought the sex provision was a "fluke . . . conceived out of wedlock." He trivialized the whole issue of sex discrimination by commenting that men were entitled to have female sec-retaries.[43]

But there were a few women attorneys who were intent on taking advantage of the new legal opportunity for job equality. One of them was Elaine Jones, a young black attorney working for the NAACP Legal Defense Fund. Looking back years later, Jones said,

> Women now had a tool . . . but then you need lawyers and you need people who are willing to complain. You need women who are willing to stand up and to say "I've been wronged and I'm going to court to vindicate my rights."[44]

The first case testing the sex provision of Title VII was not pressed by a college-educated woman bored with housewifery. Ida May Phillips, a white waitress in Florida struggling to support her seven children, saw a newspaper advertisement for trainees at the Martin Marietta Co.[45]

The company refused to even take her application, saying she should be home with her young children. But Phillips knew that she was her children's sole means of support. She could not enjoy the luxury of staying home while her family starved to death or barely sur-vived on welfare payments. The NAACP Legal Defense Fund agreed to take her case. Losing in the lower courts, they appealed to the Supreme Court. Recalling the vic-tory later, Jones smiled when she said,

> And there the Court got it right. . . . Ida May Phillips represented for us—a woman who stood up, who applied for that assembly training job, and said, "I should be treated no different from a man. I'm qualified. I can do the job, and this society should stop discriminating against me because I have borne children."

But for all the satisfaction of courtroom victories, women quickly began to realize that the law alone could not significantly change their lives. They would have to make it abundantly clear that full equality for women was no joking matter.

6

THE "MAKING IT" MYTH

I consider the right to elective abortion . . . the cornerstone of the women's movement . . . because without that right, we'd have about as many rights as the cow who is brought to the bull once a year.

—A prochoice activist before abortion was legally obtainable[1]

Ladies and gentlemen, can you believe that this pretty little thing is an assistant attorney general?"

—Said by a judge as he asked Nannette Dodge to face the courtroom in the 1980s[2]

We are used as tokens, vaunted as exceptions, while every problem that we share is treated . . . as a special case. So to those who say, "Any woman can," as if there is no such thing as discrimination, as if that were exceptional, I say this . . . all women can't. *And that will be true so long as those who do make it are the privileged few. Until all women can, none of us succeed as women, but as exceptions.*

—From a 1982 speech by attorney Catharine A. MacKinnon[3]

It was soon apparent that without a big push, the EEOC was not going to vigorously pursue the issue of sex discrimination in employment.[4] But in the 1960s, although thousands of women were playing an indispensable role in the Civil Rights and antiwar movements, writing and distributing leaflets, marching in demonstrations, and facing the same dangers in the South faced by men, their gender-programmed "roles" did not change.

Male movement leaders spoke out passionately for social justice, but they said nothing about advancing women into leadership positions instead of leaving them on the sidelines—cooking, cleaning, making coffee, and providing sexual companionship. On those occasions when women asked for the right to participate in decision making, they were usually greeted with laughter and even outright hostility.[5]

Many young lawyers, both men and women, were changed and moved by the social struggles of the 1960s. Thousands of them decided to devote their careers to poor and minority clients and/or civil rights and other social cases. Even corporate law firms, in order to attract the best of the young graduates, found it necessary to promise job applicants free time to volunteer for unpaid public interest cases.

Many older lawyers also immersed themselves in "movement" law. Mary Kaufman, the woman who had attempted to convict I. G. Farben, left private practice in 1966 when she became terribly upset by the war in Vietnam. She played an important role defending arrested civil rights and antiwar activists around the country, and training volunteer lawyers in the National Lawyers Guild's Mass Defense Office.[6]

Faced by demands for an end to the war in Vietnam and solutions to social problems, President Lyndon Baines Johnson signed the Economic Opportunity Act, launching a War on Poverty in 1964. Neighborhood-based Community Action Programs were set up in many cities. In 1966 the Supreme Court ordered mandatory, federally funded public defender systems. Within a few years, the number of lawyers available to represent poor defendants rose more than sixfold. Until then, no course on poverty law had ever been taught at a law school. But by the late 1960s, dozens were being offered to meet the needs of the many students anxious to serve as public defenders.

The director of the National Conference of Black Lawyers, Haywood Burns, commented on the impact these programs had on lawyers: "I think the southern civil rights movement pricked the conscience of a lot of lawyers. And the Legal Services program made it possible for people to do poverty law and still eat."[7]

In Community Action Program offices in poor neighborhoods, many people got together for the first time and discussed common problems. As women receiving payments from Aid for Dependent Children (AFDC) met one another, they talked about the hardships of living on welfare payments and about the indignities they suffered. They were tired of social workers showing up at their doors unannounced at any time of day or night, searching for husbands or boyfriends who might be "helping out," opening closets to look for new clothing or toys in order to prove that there was more money around than welfare provided.

Often young lawyers met with welfare recipients to advise them on their legal rights. By 1966 local welfare rights groups had founded the National Welfare Rights Organization (NWRO). After coordinated demonstrations at welfare centers in several cities in 1968, complete with sit-ins and arrests, the NWRO won numerous concessions, including extra money for necessities like winter clothing for children and *scheduled* visits from caseworkers.[8]

Welfare mothers had never had allies when their tiny subsistence checks were threatened. In late 1970, Nevada's state welfare department announced a campaign against welfare "cheaters." Without hearings or further warning, 7,000 mothers and children found empty mailboxes or reduced checks when they went looking for their rent and food money. NWRO launched Operation Nevada. Within a few weeks, welfare rights leaders, lawyers, and law students, many of them young women like Sylvia Law, who had recently graduated from NYU Law School, arrived in Nevada. They held public hearings, organized demonstrations, and filed a federal lawsuit to force the state authorities to reinstate welfare payments. In a few weeks the federal district court ordered full back payments made to everyone deprived of their rights.

By then, lawyers in several major cities were forming experimental law firms they called "law communes" to concentrate on the defense of people's political and economic rights. They planned to organize their farms democratically, with equal wages and decision-making powers for every member of the firm, instead of the highly competitive pecking order common at corporate law firms.[9]

Typical was the Law Commune in New York City, formed in 1968 when hundreds of students were arrested during antiwar protests at Columbia University. Despite the good intentions of the nineteen antiracist, antiwar men of the commune, only two women lawyers were invited to join in the project. In most other cities, women in commune offices were usually there as legal secretaries.

The women of New York's Law Commune were less than satisfied with their "equal" status. One woman member summed it up this way:

. . . at least here everybody admits that there is such a thing as chauvinism, at least verbally.

155

Other places I've worked, well, some tried to deal with it, but in most, either the man would say, "Forget it, I'm not a chauvinist" or "I am but it doesn't matter.". . . It's hard for them [women] to be on the same competitive level as a man. Men are told all along that the best possible thing for them is to be famous, to be a star. . . . The profession offers an incentive to be a male chauvinist. You get points as a lawyer for being competitive, aggressive, famous, for destroying the other side—so it's hard to be schizophrenic, to be one way in court and another outside of it.[10]

Women's law communes did not form until a few years later. Most women attorneys continued to take jobs in Legal Services offices where many women worked and the atmosphere was more congenial. A few were even put in charge. Carol Ruth Silver, a graduate of the University of Chicago Law School, who spent more than a month in a jail in Mississippi during the 1961 Freedom Rides, eventually become executive director of the Berkeley Neighborhood Legal Services program.

By then a new women's rights movement was in the early stages of development. While they were involved in campaigns against the war, for minority rights, and poor people's legal rights, women activists were quietly getting together to discuss their special problems. It was one thing to discuss employment and educational discrimination, but many of them had never openly talked about the deep dark secrets of rape, sexual harassment, wife battering, and illegal abortions.

The more women raised these issues, the more they realized they needed a movement of their own. The feminist movement of the early part of the century began to show signs of awakening from its fifty-year Rip Van Winkle nap. Women law students and lawyers played an important role in that wake-up call.

First there were scattered rebellions here and there. On Ladies' Day at Harvard in 1968, eight women showed up at their property law class prepared to present a moot court (practice) case. As usual, the professor had chosen embarrassing "stolen property"— ladies' lingerie.

The women filed into class dressed like male attorneys—all in black, wearing horn-rim glasses and carrying briefcases. At the appropriate moment for presenting the "evidence," they simultaneously opened their briefcases and showered the professor with frilly underwear. It was the last Ladies Day at Harvard.[11]

In a more serious vein, at the American Civil Liberties Union, three women lawyers, Faith Seidenberg, Pauli Murray, a black civil rights attorney, and Dorothy Kenyon asked the ruling Board of the ACLU to finance a Women's Rights Project, specifically to press cases for women's rights to equal protection guaranteed under the Fourteenth Amendment. Ruth Bader Ginsburg, a volunteer at ACLU, became director of the project. Ginsburg argued half a dozen cases before the nine justices of the U.S. Supreme Court, probably never dreaming that someday she would be seated among them.

In the District of Columbia, volunteer women lawyers founded the Women's Legal Defense Fund (WLDF), which eventually would bring about recognition of sexual harassment as a violation of Title VII. Women law students at New York University formed the Women's Rights Committee. They won their first legal battle in 1969, making a prestigious for-men-only scholarship available to women. Through their efforts, the first Women in Law course in the nation was introduced at NYU.

In the fall of 1969, women law students at NYU and Columbia University joined together and threatened to sue a large New York law firm that refused to even schedule interviews with women graduates. Undoubtedly to avoid court action, the firm reversed its policy "as a courtesy."

Columbia Law School established an Employment Rights Project, with federal EEOC funding, and filed a class-action lawsuit on behalf of all women applicants against another large law firm in 1971, hoping to set a precedent. Constance Baker Motley, the only woman judge in the federal court of New York State, was assigned to the case. Lawyers from the large firm attempted to have Motley disqualified for bias (as a woman) against the defendant. When the law firm lost its appeal, it settled and signed a new set of hiring guidelines.

Winning a case here and a case there, just as suffragists had won voting rights in a few states before 1920, women found progress painfully slow. Law firms hired women by ones and twos but informed them that they would never become partners in the firm. Other female professionals, and advocates for abortion rights and welfare rights, as well as women who were pushing for genuine equality in job opportunities, decided to do what participants in every other movement in the sixties had done—join together and march to show their strength.

On August 26, 1970, fifty years to the day after women won the right to vote, 100,000 women marched down Fifth Avenue in New York City carrying signs with demands ranging from legal abortion to equal job opportunities and child care centers.

The press had not dared to ridicule the Civil Rights Movement or even the welfare rights movement, but just as it had mocked the early suffragists and called them "she-males," so now it had a field day with the new women's movement. When a small group of feminists, tired of being defined by their hairdos, clothes, and body parts, burned brassieres at an Atlantic City Miss America contest, the entire movement and all of its urgent demands were reduced by the press to a "bra-burning brigade of lesbians."

In the surge of this second wave of feminism, a number of women lawyers decided to form their own law firms. Over the next few years these firms filed many successful sex discrimination suits in the communications industry. Women lawyers even sued a bank to help married women establish their own credit. But these lawyers soon faced serious economic problems, just as women in law had in the past. Because they often worked to defend poor women for low fees, refused cases that contradicted their feminist ideals, and took Title VII cases that sometimes dragged on for years before a penny of income came into the firm, most women's law communes by the late 1970s could no longer stay in business.

One woman lawyer gaining her credentials in those days was Hillary Diane Rodham, later to be First Lady Hillary Rodham Clinton. A firm believer in racial equality and women's equal rights,[12] Rodham graduated from Wellesley in 1969 as the women's movement was becoming more visible. Told by a Harvard professor, "We don't need any more women," Rodham went on to Yale Law School, where she met Bill Clinton. After graduation she studied child development and family law for a year and then joined the Children's Defense Fund. In 1973 she spent six months as legal counsel to the House Judiciary Committee investigating the Watergate scandal that led to President Nixon's resignation. In 1974, Hillary Rodham moved to Arkansas with Bill Clinton, where she taught law for several years and in 1980 became a senior litigating partner at the Rose Law Firm in Little Rock. As a director on three major corporate boards, she worked to convince large corporations like Wal-Mart to hire and promote women and minorities.

In 1970 a well-known figure in the women's movement, New York lawyer Bella Abzug, ran for Congress. "Nobody had ever run on a women's rights plank," Abzug later told an interviewer. Her campaign slogan was: "This woman's place is in the house—the House of Representatives." Abzug won the election and continued to speak out on women's rights in Congress. President Carter fired Abzug as head of the Women's Commission in 1979 because, Abzug explained, the Commission argued with Carter over budget cuts affecting women.

> Our committee said to him, "You can't cut the little women have in the budget. The majority of women in this country are suffering. They are the majority of the poor, the majority of the unemployed, the majority of the old; they can hardly survive in this period of economic crisis." Carter's answer was that economic policies were not women's issues.[13]

Despite all these efforts, the number of women law students had increased in the early 1970s to only 9 percent nationally. In 1971, only 70 women registered at Harvard Law School in a class of 563, the first time any class was more than 10 percent female. A decade later in 1981, at a class reunion, two members of that class interviewed most of the women to record their recollections of college and learn what had happened to them since.[14]

The women remembered their law school experience as something of a nightmare. The attitudes of Harvard administrators, teachers, and students had not changed very much since the 1950s, when less than a dozen women were entering the law school each year. On bathroom walls and in passageways, ugly graffiti portrayed the Harvard law coeds as fat monsters with acne and hairy armpits. "Because we were fledgling lawyers, we weren't women," one alumna said.[15]

Although some younger professors supported women's rights, many older professors refused to modify their

Bella Abzug (in hat) ran for Congress and won in 1970
with the campaign slogan: "This woman's place is in the house—
the House of Representatives." Abzug is shown here
marching with fellow feminists.

behavior. The atmosphere at the law school was ruthlessly competitive for all of the students. Those with the highest first-year grades made *Law Review* status, a major step toward future career success. There were no makeup examinations, not even for illness. A higher percentage of women than men finished their first year in the top tenth of the class. Since women were only 10 percent of entering students, they were the cream of the crop of all women college graduates. Less competitive than the men, they also gave one another considerable support, organizing a group called "Freaked out Friends," where they discussed their problems on the campus and women's issues in general.

The women's liberation movement had considerable impact on all of them, although only a few, like Marley Sue Weiss, spoke out regularly in class, protesting sexist language in case study presentations. Weiss had been a founding member of a women's liberation group at Barnard College. At Harvard she helped organize the Women's Law Association (WLA). WLA campaigned for a myriad of changes, from more women's bathrooms to an increase in the number of women admitted and the hiring of women law professors. As to the last demand, the administration claimed it could not find a qualified woman teacher. Actually, the previous year Ruth Bader Ginsburg, the future Supreme Court justice, had taught a Women in the Law course at Harvard, yet was not invited to teach full-time. When Columbia Law School offered her a permanent tenured position, she dropped her efforts at Harvard.

In 1972, Title IX of the Education Amendments Act forbade discrimination in educational programs receiving federal funds. Law school admissions and placement offices were pressured to obey the law and make sure that more women were admitted and that equal employment opportunities existed for those who graduated and passed the bar examination. With law firms under legal pressure to hire more women, many of the women at Harvard decided to try to make it in the male-dominated business law world.

Nevertheless, about thirty of them volunteered to spend twenty hours a week at the Harvard Legal Aid Bureau helping indigent Boston clients. Some later said that this work in the real world kept them from dropping out of school. A surprising half of the volunteers decided to make careers in public interest and poverty law. Some were bluntly told that they were wasting a space at Harvard that could have gone to someone interested in "real law."

Despite such pressures, most of the volunteers continued this work after graduation. Judy Berkan moved to Puerto Rico in 1977, where she defended political activists. Marley Sue Weiss's first job was dispensing legal advice for the United Auto Workers union, and several other Harvard women worked as public defenders.

Those who decided to compete with men for top positions found the job search unequal but improved by 1974. They obtained positions with prestigious law firms, but almost always they were alone—token women to satisfy legal requirements. Above them was what came to be called a "glass ceiling," an invisible barrier of prejudice that meant they would never become a partner in the firm. It wasn't until 1984 that the Supreme Court, in *Hishon* v. *King and Spalding*, ruled that law firms could be sued under Title VII for denial of partnership status on the basis of sex.

While the women of Harvard's class of 1974 struggled to complete law school, the abortion issue became the main focus of the women's liberation movement. Until 1969, legal abortion was unavailable in the United States. Even in states with liberal laws, a doctor could perform the procedure only on women who had been raped, were victims of incest, or were in danger of death if they continued their pregnancies.

Each year thousands of desperate women slipped off to lower-priced back-alley abortionists for unsafe procedures. Many of them were injured or even lost their lives. Safe abortions were available only to women with enough money to travel to countries where abortion was legal, but most women could not afford these alternatives. In the United States organized crime had a stable of doctors performing expensive abortions under its protection. The 1970 Nixon Report on Crime listed illegal abortions as the third highest moneymaker for the Mafia.

One women's statement, reprinted at the start of this chapter, reflected the feelings of millions of others who considered the right to abortion the most important right of all. A two-pronged fight in the courtroom and in the streets was launched to legalize abortion. As lawyers, the majority of them women, took cases to state courts, movement activists held hearings, set up information booths in public places, lobbied state legislators, and marched and rallied in major cities.

In 1969, by a 4 to 3 vote, the California Supreme Court reversed the conviction of a doctor for performing an abortion and declared the restrictive state law unconstitutional. Citing "the Supreme Court's and this Court's repeated acknowledgment of a 'right of privacy' and of liberty in matters related to marriage, family, and sex," California's highest court declared that women had "the fundamental right . . . to choose whether to bear children."

The "right to choose" became the slogan of the women's liberation movement. Opponents of legal abortion defended the fetus's "right to life." Supporters of the right to choose pointed out that right-to-life advocates had nothing to say about babies killed by bombs in Vietnam or the welfare of children from poor families.

New York, Hawaii, and Alaska repealed laws prohibiting abortion, but in every other state they remained in force. So the fight continued. In Texas, a twenty-seven-year-old woman lawyer, Sarah Weddington, became involved in a case that would make history.[16] Weddington was by no means an activist in the social movements of the 1960s. The daughter of a minister, she grew up in a small West Texas town with conventional ideas about women's roles. At a small Methodist college in Abilene, Weddington decided to go on to law school. The dean advised against it, insisting that law school would be too demanding for a woman.

Perhaps to prove him wrong, Sarah Weddington applied and was accepted by the University of Texas School of Law in Austin in June 1965. She was one of five women among 120 men in her entering class. At school, she met and fell in love with Ron Weddington. With three years of law school ahead, they decided to postpone marriage until after graduation. In 1967, Sarah found out that she was pregnant and decided that an abortion was the only way that she and Ron could stay in school. Later she described the terrible ordeal of "a scared graduate student in 1967 in a dirty dusty Mexican border town to have an abortion, fleeing the law that made abortion illegal in Texas."[17]

In 1968 Ron and Sarah married. While her husband continued his studies, Sarah went out job hunting. She met the usual fate of women lawyers searching for their first job—no offers—until one of her professors offered her a temporary research position.

By then the Berkeley Free Speech movement had spread to Austin and the campus bustled with civil rights and antiwar activity as well as a fledgling women's movement. Sarah Weddington started attending what the women called their "consciousness raising sessions." Soon the group published a guide to places where safe abortions were available and started a referral project.

Worried that they could be arrested for their activities, Weddington researched the legal issues involved.

In the law library she stumbled across the Supreme Court's Griswold decision regarding birth control that she believed was applicable to the issue of abortion rights. If the Court considered contraception a personal matter in which the government had no right to interfere, Weddington reasoned, the abortion decision should be in the same category. She decided to file a lawsuit challenging Texas's antiabortion statute, but she needed a client—a pregnant woman brave enough to take her case to court.

Norma McCorvey agreed to file suit as "Jane Roe" against Henry Wade, the district attorney of Dallas County for thirty-five years and a committed foe of legal abortion. In June 1970, after Weddington and McCorrey had lost in the lower courts, the Texas State Supreme Court ruled in favor of "Roe." Commenting on the decision, a *New York Times* editorial stated, "It certainly proves that genteel southern ladies can be very good lawyers."[18]

Wade immediately announced that he would appeal the decision. Meanwhile, lawyers were taking on similar cases in other states.[19] It was almost certain that one of these cases would come before the Supreme Court, making abortion either legal or illegal throughout the nation.

On December 13, 1971, four attorneys waited in the Supreme Court building in Washington, D.C., ready to argue their cases. Because three of them were women, many lawyers referred to December 13 as Ladies' Day. Weddington noticed that "ladies" were not frequent visitors to the building. The rest rooms were all marked "Men," and all of the justices were also male.

The Court chose to review *Roe* v. *Wade* but delayed its decision for over a year. On January 22, 1973, the Supreme Court avoided the constitutional issues and ruled that "the abortion decision and its effectuation must be left to the *medical judgment of the pregnant woman's attending physician.*" (Italics added.) The decision also allowed states to place limitations on abortion. The right to choose had been tentatively won, but the door had been left open for an all-out legal war to minimize its impact.

After the *Roe* v. *Wade* victory, the largest women's organization, the National Organization of Women (NOW) decided to devote most of its attention to ratification of the Equal Rights Amendment (ERA), which would automatically strike down all state laws discriminating against women.[20] Some women in NOW thought that since many laws had already been changed, the energies of the women's movement should be turned instead to issues like day-care centers and health care for all, but they were outvoted.

In 1972 ERA had been passed by both houses of Congress, but thirty-eight states had to ratify the amendment before it could be an official part of the Constitution. Despite an extension on the seven-year deadline, ERA was defeated three states short of ratification. A worn-out women's rights movement once more left the streets, returning only when the right to choose came under sharp attack. As the economy declined, poor women—black, Latina, and white—saw day-care centers close and their conditions worsen. No viable movement existed to help them fight for their right to survive.

Almost immediately after the *Roe* v. *Wade* decision, several states passed restrictive legislation requiring the consent of husbands and even the parents of unmarried minors or requiring doctors to attempt to talk women out of an abortion decision by graphically describing the stages of fetal development. "The states are not free," declared Supreme Court Justice Harry Blackmun, "under the guise of protecting maternal health or potential life, to intimidate women into continuing pregnancies."

In 1976 Congress passed the Hyde amendment, banning the use of Medicaid funds (federal money designated for the health care of the poor) for abortions, except in cases where the mother's life was endangered. When opponents of the amendment tried to at least allow payment for abortions for rape victims, they were told that rape almost never caused pregnancy and that women would pretend they were raped in order to receive a paid abortion.[21]

When the law was legally challenged and the case reached the Supreme Court, the conservative majority on the Court ruled the Hyde amendment legal. Three justices dissented. One of them, Thurgood Marshall, the only African American justice on the Court, wrote a powerful minority opinion opposing the decision.

> The class burdened by the Hyde Amendment consists of indigent women, a substantial proportion of whom are members of minority races. . . . There is another world "out there," the existence of which the Court either chooses to ignore or fears to recognize. In my view, it is only by blinding itself to that other world that the Court can reach the result it announces today.[22]

In 1989, under continued pressure from the women's movement, Congress voted to restore funding in cases of rape or incest, but President George Bush vetoed the legislation. The Hyde amendment was repealed shortly after Bill Clinton took office in 1992.

Laws relating to the crime of rape were another "unmentionable" issue that women lawyers tackled head on. In many states a witness was required in order to convict a rapist, although everyone realized the improbability of a rapist's committing his crime in front of others! In other places a rape victim had to prove "earnest resistance," even if she had been threatened with a deadly weapon. Lawyers defending accused rapists were allowed to ask victims about their sex lives and comment on their morals and even the way they looked. Many women apparently hid the fact that they had'been raped for fear that they would be humiliated and treated like criminals.

Not surprisingly, the *California Law Review* in 1973 stated that "a man who rapes a woman who reports the crime to police has roughly seven chances out of eight of walking away without a conviction."[23]

In New Mexico, Connie K. Borkenhagen urged the state legislature to change the laws regarding rape trials. To make her point she told the story of a robbery victim hypothetically cross examined by a lawyer the way a rape victim is questioned.

> "Mr. Smith, you were held up at gunpoint on the corner of First and Main?"
> "Yes."
> "Did you struggle with the robber?"
> "No."
> "Why not?"
> "He was armed."
> "Then you made a conscious decision to comply with his demands rather than resist?"
> "Yes."
> "Did you scream? Cry out?"
> "No. I was afraid."
> "I see. Have you ever been held up before?"
> "No."
> "Have you ever given money away?"
> "Yes, of course."
> "And you did so willingly?"
> "What are you getting at?"
> "Well let's put it like this, Mr. Smith. You've given

money away in the past. In fact, you have quite a reputation for philanthropy. How can we be sure you weren't contriving to have your money taken from you by force?"[24]

Laws were gradually changed, but as late as 1989 a jury in a rape trial in Fort Lauderdale, Florida, found a man accused of raping a woman repeatedly at knifepoint not guilty because "it felt she was up to no good the way she was dressed."

Women attorneys created a new vocabulary for other unspoken crimes against women. Until very recently, the law had little to say about wife beating and even less to say about men harassing women at work with sexual innuendos and insults. These crimes at last were given names: "wife battering" and "sexual harassment." Under persistent pressure from the women's movement, laws were passed to punish those who committed these crimes. However, the reactions of judges to rape, domestic violence, and sexual harassment seemed to vary widely according to the sex of the judge. "I think seventy to eighty percent of men don't believe charges of battering, and all women think it's worse than charged," one woman judge told author Mona Harrington.[25]

In 1994, some 250 federal judges attending the annual convention of the National Association of Women Judges heard a report that indicated that gender bias was still rampant in the judicial system. In juvenile courts, male judges often sentenced girls to longer periods of detention because they felt "boys will be boys and girls ought to behave like little ladies." They also more frequently ordered psychiatric examinations "for women claiming sexual harassment, but not for men who charge race or age discrimination."[26]

Women became acutely aware of these less than objective differences in male-female attitudes during the confirmation hearings for Supreme Court nominee

Clarence Thomas in 1993. A black woman law professor, Anita Hill, who had worked for Thomas, testified that he had sexually harassed her over a long period of time. The senators on the Judiciary Committee were all male, and the "all-white, all-male panel clearly could not, or would not, comprehend Hill's story."[27] Some observers thought that they glossed over Hill's charges because they believed in the "boys will be boys" mentality. Others alleged more sinister motives.

By the mid-1980s and mid-1990s, civil rights and women's rights advocates fought simply to "run in place" in an economy that appeared to be in a permanent slump. For African American and Latina women in the field of law, the gains had been modest.

In 1970, black and Latino lawyers of both sexes composed only 1.3 percent of all lawyers and there were only about 800 nonwhite law students out of 65,000 in the nation. After the Supreme Court ordered affirmative action programs in 1976, more nonwhite students were admitted to law schools, but they found themselves at a severe disadvantage. Many of them had attended inferior ghetto high schools and found law school extremely difficult. Out of those who completed their studies, their pass rates on the bar exam were barely half that for whites. Only a few were hired by law firms—to fulfill legal requirements—so most took public defender and other government jobs.

Black women did a little better in the private job market than black men. To satisfy affirmative action guidelines for the hiring of women and racial minorities, many firms turned to a two-for-the-price-of-one scheme. They hired *one* new associate who fulfilled both race and sex requirements for *one* salary—a black woman. Sometimes they opted for a three-for-one candidate—a black Latina woman. In any case, many African American and Latina women lawyers often preferred to work in situations where they could help other blacks and Latinos.

Anita Hill smiles during Clarence Thomas's
confirmation hearing when Senator Howell Heflin
asks her if she has a "martyr's complex."

Sheila Rush Okpaku certainly could have been a likely candidate to fulfill a large law firm's affirmative action requirements when she graduated from Harvard Law School in 1964, the only African American in a group of four or five women in a class of 400. Instead, she went to work for the NAACP Legal Defense and Educational Fund.

Okpaku quickly "became disillusioned with test cases, and their effect on poor and black people." In 1968, she went to work as associate director of the Community Law Office (CLO) in Harlem and East Harlem, New York City's largest black and Latino ghettos. The CLO had been organized during a tenant-landlord dispute in Harlem, when a group of volunteer lawyers from Wall Street firms set up a free legal clinic in the neighborhood. CLO was determined to provide "the kind of legal representation that has heretofore been limited to the rich . . . instead of the spotty help of most Legal Aid programs or the often mass production representation of Legal Services programs." Okpaku became director of CLO in 1971.[28]

Other black women lawyers went to work for the government in hopes of having long-lasting power to change and enforce the laws that affected black people. Eleanor Holmes Norton, born in 1933, grew up in Washington, D.C. Angry about segregation, she remembered that she "could not understand why black people were abiding this treatment . . . it was almost embarrassing to me that there was not a civil rights movement."[29] In 1970 Mayor John V. Lindsay appointed Norton as head of the New York City Commission on Human Rights, and from there she was appointed to head the U.S. Equal Employment Opportunity Commission. Norton successfully reduced a logjam of 70,000 neglected discrimination cases involving minorities and women.

Barbara Jordan, born into a poor family in Texas in the middle of the Great Depression, worked her way through college and Boston University Law School. In 1965, Jordan became the first black woman elected to the Texas State Legislature. In 1972 she was elected to the U.S. Congress, where she worked hard for the benefit of the black, Latino, and white working-class people of her district.

Patricia Roberts Harris became the first black woman in a presidential cabinet when she was named secretary of Housing and Urban Development by President Jimmy Carter in 1977; she became secretary of Health, Education, and Welfare in 1980. Harris had attended Howard University and participated in the 1943 desegregation sit-ins in Washington. At her Senate confirmation hearings for the post of secretary of Housing and Urban Development, Senator William Proxmire asked her if she would "really make an effort to get the views of those who are less articulate and less likely to be knocking on your door with outstanding credentials?" Harris answered:

> Senator, I am one of them. You do not seem to understand who I am. I am a black women, the daughter of a dining-car waiter. I am a black woman who even eight years ago could not buy a house in some parts of the District of Columbia. . . . I assure you that while there may be those who forget what it meant to be excluded from the dining room of this very building, I shall not forget.[30]

Constance Baker Motley also chose the route of political office, first being elected to the New York State Senate and in 1965 becoming borough president of Manhattan, the first black woman in either post. In 1966 Motley became the first black woman to sit on the U.S. District Court for the Southern District of New York State. In 1980 she became chief judge of the court.

174

Representative Barbara Jordan addresses a Democratic
Party panel. Co-panelists include Senator Stuart Symington
(center) of Missouri and Senator (later vice president)
Walter Mondale (right) of Minnesota.

Although most of the first group of pioneer Latina attorneys earned their degrees after the socially conscious days of the 1960s, almost all of them focused their careers on the task of improving conditions for poorer Latinos.[31] Antonia Hernández is one example. She arrived in the East Los Angeles barrio (neighborhood) with her Mexican parents when she was eight, suffering in schools where bilingual programs did not exist.[32] She decided to become a lawyer in order to change the laws that were holding back Latino children. In 1981 she became a staff attorney for the Mexican American Legal Defense Fund (MALDEF), promoting affirmative action and bilingual programs.

Less than 300 Latina lawyers have been appointed or elected as judges, but many of them have handed out social justice along with legal justice. Petra Jimenez Maes, like so many women lawyers before her, started her law career by offering free legal services to New Mexico's poor. Appointed to fill a state district court vacancy in 1981, Jimenez Maes was elected for a new term and in 1984 established New Mexico's first family court. She was awarded MALDEF's Distinguished Service Award for her development of programs to help the youth brought into her courtroom. Likewise, Myrna Milan, the first Latina appointed as a municipal court judge in Newark, New Jersey, created an alternative sentence program for young offenders.

Irma Vidal Santaella, the original pioneer Latina attorney, was appointed to the New York State Supreme Court in 1983 (see Chapter 5).

Carmen Beauchamp Ciparick, the daughter of Puerto Rican immigrants, in 1993 became the first woman appointed to New York State's highest court—the Court of Appeals. In a landmark decision as state Supreme Court judge in 1990, she ruled that a state program to provide prenatal care for the working poor was unconstitutional because it excluded abortions.[33]

Patricia Roberts Harris, who served as secretary of Housing
and Urban Development and secretary of Health, Education,
and Welfare, was the first black woman in a presidential cabinet.

Despite the increase in their numbers, very few women lawyers have practiced as private criminal attorneys.[34] More have been seen in courtrooms, however, as Title VII has made it possible for them to win jobs as district attorneys and public defenders. It remains difficult for any woman attorney, no matter how competent, to find paying clients for a private practice. Many people accused of crimes, whatever their race or sex, may realize that white male lawyers are more likely to have all-important connections with judges and prosecutors.

But when male criminal lawyers are asked why they think this gender gap exists, they continue to insist that women lack "the necessary combative nature in the courtroom" and that "once before a judge, a women's self-confidence and intelligence would quickly evaporate." Anyway, they often add, women want it that way to avoid "sleazy clientele" and "possible physical risks."[35]

Few male attorneys ever mention the behavior of judges toward women attorneys as a possible stumbling block for women's "self-confidence." One woman attorney, Alice McClanahan, minces no words when she lectures law students on the problems women lawyers continue to face in the courtroom.

> You will meet with rudeness, be patronized, swept aside and often have to fight for the merest right. You will find judges inclined to give the best of an argument to your male opponents. You will be condescended to, ignored, and you will have to fight every step of the way.[36]

Many judges have seemed incapable of accepting women lawyers. In Texas, one judge in the 1980s asked Nannette Dodge to face the courtroom and then said, "Ladies and gentlemen, can you believe that this pretty little thing is an assistant attorney general?"[37]

Watergate prosecutor Jill Wine Volner coined a name for this not uncommon behavior: "sexual trial tactics." Even during the Watergate hearings, wearying of the put-down "compliments" of H. R. Haldeman's lawyer, John J. Wilson, Volner told him that "if he didn't stop I'd have to lower myself to his level and respond in kind."

In 1982, trial lawyer Elizabeth C. Kaming had an entire panel of jurors excused because of repeated sexist remarks by the opposing counsel. In Nassau County Supreme Court, Judge Anthony Jordan frequently addressed lawyer Martha Coppleman as "little girl."[38]

Even in the mid-1980s, the chief prosecutor in a federal district court publicly stated, "When you're fighting a war against crime, you don't send a girl into the front lines."[39] It seems unlikely that he had ever heard of Elizabeth Holtzman, who had been elected and reelected as a hard-hitting district attorney in Brooklyn, New York.

A few good men stepped in to do something about this "special treatment" received by women attorneys. When Newark, New Jersey, judge Marilyn Loftus talked about the problem to Robert N. Wilentz, chief justice of the New Hampshire Supreme Court, he created a Task Force on Women in the Courts. The results of the Task Force study, issued in 1983, supported Loftus's concerns. Eighty-six percent of the lawyers surveyed stated that many lawyers made insulting jokes about women in the courtroom, and two-thirds said judges were also guilty of similar behavior. In his own courtroom, Justice Wilentz made it clear that he would not permit such behavior, but this did not solve the problem in thousands of other courts.

The National Organization of Women's Legal Defense Fund has financed the National Judicial Education Program to Promote Equality for Women and Men in the Courts. Teams of lawyers offer training session to judges on recognizing and dealing with "sexual trial tactics."

Despite many efforts to equalize the situation, women trial lawyers remain a small minority. In many places, women judges are still considered unusual. When Susie M. Sharp was appointed to the North Carolina state court, one journalist asked her if a rape case "wouldn't be too much for her delicate sensibilities." Like so many women judges before her, Sharp's answer was laced with angry wit: "In the first place, there could have been no rape had not a woman been present, and I consider it eminently fitting that one be in on the 'pay-off,'" she retorted.[40] In January 1975 Sharp became chief justice of the court.

Some newspaper reporters pose questions to women judges that they would never have dared ask a male judge. Judge Birdie Amsterdam, asked by an interviewer how she could work in court without a ladies' room for judges, wittily responded, "I have learned how to steel myself so that I no longer require a bathroom between the hours of nine and five."[41]

Rude questions were nothing compared to the treatment received by Rose Elizabeth Bird in 1977, when she was named chief justice of the state of California. Opponents organized several unsuccessful recall campaigns to remove her from the bench, and as she drove around her state, she often saw bumper stickers reading "Bye Bye Birdie."

In reality, only a handful of women have been appointed or elected to high state courts, usually in places where the women's movement has remained active. In Madison, Wisconsin, a college town with a long history of peace movement and women's liberation activism, Judge Archie Simonson sentenced a teenage boy who attacked a young girl in a high school stairwell to probation, suggesting that the boy had reacted "normally" to provocative dress and a climate

Rose Elizabeth Bird lost her bid to be reelected
as chief justice of the California Supreme Court.

of sexual permissiveness. A movement formed that organized demonstrations and won a recall election. Maria Krueger, a public defender, ran successfully against Judge Simonson in 1977.

The National Association of Women Judges was founded in 1979 to deal with the problems faced by women on the bench.[42] Along with women attorneys, its members pressed for the appointment of women to higher-ranking federal judgeships and even for the Supreme Court to break its all-male tradition. Richard Nixon had made four Supreme Court appointments before he resigned in disgrace during the Watergate scandal in 1973. Although under pressure from the women's movement, he claimed that he could not find a qualified woman "good enough." Congresswoman Bella Abzug quipped that Nixon could not find one "bad enough."[43]

Although President Jimmy Carter appointed forty-one women to the federal bench, it barely made a dent. By the end of Carter's term, out of more than 20,000 appointed judgeships, only 900 were held by women. It was Carter's successor, Ronald Reagan, who appointed the first woman Supreme Court associate justice, Sandra Day O'Connor, in 1981!

President Reagan was fulfilling a pledge made during the 1980 election campaign, when many women opposed him because of his open opposition to the Equal Rights Amendment. To counter their resentment, he had pledged that he would fill "one of the first Supreme Court vacancies" with "the most qualified woman." During Senate confirmation hearings, feminist groups were reassured when O'Conner said that although she found abortion "offensive," she "felt obligated to recognize that others have different views."[44]

In 1989, *Time* magazine claimed that "women are riding a new wave of dominium."[45] In public places like the Supreme Court building, things certainly appeared to have changed. By 1986, over a third of the law clerks were women. Sixteen years earlier they had been a mere 3 percent. Women were no longer "rare birds" on the campuses of law schools either. At many universities they composed up to 40 percent of the law student body. But a closer look revealed some dismaying facts.

In 1991, Susan Faludi wrote a much publicized book providing evidence that "breathless reports about droves of female 'careerists' crashing the legal, medical, and other elite professions were inflated."[46] Most of the progress was made at the height of the women's movement, fifteen years earlier. Progress peaked in the early 1980s and "barely budged since," Faludi pointed out. Between 1972 and 1988, women had increased their share of professional jobs by only 5 percent, she claimed.

The "Equal Employment Opportunity File" of the Census Bureau was not released until 1993, and then only on CD-ROM.[47] The little publicized data more than back up Faludi's thesis. It revealed that less than one-third of all lawyers in the United States were women. (Male total, 564,332; female total, 182,745.)

Far fewer members of minority groups, male or female, had advanced during the "new wave of dominion." The Bureau of the Census categorizes racial/ethnic minorities in the professions according to their percentage of the population. The term *underrepresented* indicates that the percentage of a particular group in a professional category is less than its percentage of the population. The Hispanic and African American population groups each composes close to 12 percent of the total population, but only about 2.5 percent of the legal profession! After the initial push for equality in the 1960s and 1970s, the modest advances made by Latinos and African Americans actually declined in the late 1980s and 1990s![48]

Latina women fared even worse than Latino men. Of almost 800,000 lawyers nationally, less than 17,000 are Latino, including less than 4,000 women. The situation was only slightly better for African American attorneys. There were 14,360 African American male attorneys in 1990 and 11,310 African American females. Since each group composes about 12 percent of the population, fair representation would mean that these numbers would have to double for both African Americans and Latinos. Instead they were slowly declining as economic hard times made it more difficult to attend college. "Asians and Pacific Islanders," no longer considered an underrepresented minority in the health professions and often touted as the "model minority," were underrepresented in the legal profession.[49]

Just about the same situation applies to judges. There were about 32,000 male judges and 7,400 female judges in 1990. Among these groups, 871 of the women and 1,407 of the men were African American; among Latinos only 298 females and 800 males held elected or appointed judicial posts. There are 74 Asian women and 206 Asian men on the bench.

Census data do not reveal the status of judges or law teachers. Full professors are counted along with instructors as "secondary school law teachers." It is well known that women almost always fill the lower-status ranks in both groups, but even if we assumed equal status for all, there were 3,158 males and 1,397 females in this broad category. White females held 1,291 of these posts, black females only 70, Hispanics only 23, and Asians 29.

Except in response to attacks on legal abortion, women have stopped marching, and the few gains they have made are rapidly eroding. Congress passed the Equal Pay Act in the early 1960s, but by the mid-1990s, women still earned less than 70 cents for every dollar earned by men, and the situation was worsening![50]

Many ways have been found to "legally" pay women less for their "equal work." Women usually are hired in lower-paying departments of corporations, as communications, rather than finance, executives, for example. Even when women are partners in large law firms, they usually handle taxes or estates instead of being assigned to high-profile cases with large bonuses attached. The claim is often made that women are given less prestigious assignments because employers worry that they will leave their jobs to raise a family. But the Labor Department has reported that "within educational categories, men earn more than women at every age."

The economic policies of the Reagan and Bush administrations—"Reaganomics"—favored finance, insurance, and real estate moguls. The tycoons in these sectors were almost always men. As the dollar gap spread between the poor, the middle class, and the wealthy, the gap between men and women also widened. As one Harvard economist expressed it, "From '73 to '91 only the people at the top did extremely well—and the people at the top were predominantly male."

In 1993, a *Newsweek* article declared:

It's still a statistical piece of cake being a white man, at least in comparison with being anything else. White males make up just 39.2 percent of the population, yet they account for 82.5 percent of the Forbes 400 (folks worth at least 265 million), 77 percent of Congress, 92 percent of state governors, 70 percent of tenured college faculty, almost 90 percent of daily-newspaper editors, 77 percent of TV news directors.[51]

No doubt, many women voted for Bill Clinton when he ran for president in 1992 because of his promises on women's rights as well as Hillary Rodham Clinton's well-known positions on feminist issues. As president, Clinton reversed many of the decisions of the Bush administration, including the Hyde amendment. With an administration once again friendly toward women's rights, more women were appointed to government jobs and judicial posts.

But the same problem faced high-ranking women as faced those in private jobs. Women were still considered the main marriage partner responsible for child care. In 1993 Clinton nominated Zoe Baird for attorney general. She lost the nomination when it was discovered that she had once hired an "undocumented" immigrant (without legal papers) as a live-in nanny. No man had ever been questioned on that issue. Kimba Wood's nomination for a federal district court judgeship was withdrawn on the same basis. Finally, Janet Reno, a single woman with no children, was confirmed as attorney general.

Some women lawyers have focused on the issue of women's special role in the legal profession. Catharine A. MacKinnon, a legal scholar and ardent feminist, has long fought for laws against sexual harassment and pornography. She is especially eager for women to realize that the few women who are appointed to high posts still have an obligation to remain involved with women's problems. When Rosalie Wahl and Mary Jeane Coyne were named as associate justices of the Minnesota Supreme Court in 1982, MacKinnon made a speech at an event honoring them.

There was a danger, MacKinnon warned, that people with no real interest in women's equality would point to a few women in positions of power and say, "She made it, why can't you?"

> We are used as tokens, vaunted as exceptions, while every problem that we share is treated . . . as a special case. So to those who say, "Any woman can," as if there is no such thing as discrimination, as if that were exceptional, I say this, and I say it as a woman: all women can't.

And that will be true so long as those who do make it are the privileged few. Until all women can, none of us succeed as women, but as exceptions.[52]

MacKinnon went on to ask whether the two new state Supreme Court justices would "use the tools of law as women, for all women." She pointed out that "the definition of women in law and in life is not ours. . . . We are not allowed to be women on our own terms."

A decade later, Mona Harrington in a 1994 book on the role of women attorneys tried to answer the question, "How are women lawyers using the authority they have to advance the equality of women in general?"[53] Harrington interviewed over a hundred women lawyers of different ages. In 1985, Ronald Chester had worried that despite the advances of women lawyers in the 1980s, difficult economic times could cause "a return to the marginality" of bygone eras.[54] But Harrington discovered that Chester had missed another important issue. Many of those who did "make it" were unhappy and wanted to leave!

Harrington confirmed that the "authority structure" in the law profession had changed very little, with only about 10 percent of women lawyers working as federal and state judges, law partners, or tenured professors at high-ranking law schools. But she also discovered that Ivy League women graduates were finding it easier to land jobs in large law firms.

As more corporations had spread out over the world, many law firms serving them also became gigantic megafirms, with branch offices and thousands of lawyers. To avoid lawsuits and out of real need, these institutions soon had a 40 to 50 percent female share of new associates. For many women the financial temptation was irresistible. By 1990 a new associate made more than a new partner had made a decade earlier.

But new women associates found themselves in a male world ruled by competitiveness and overwork, where their performance was judged by "billable hours" (the hours of work the lawyers submit bills for). "Making partner" meant little recreation or time with their families. Many of the women lawyers had small children or wanted families. Some functioned like superwomen, trying to be perfect wives and mothers, while still competing with the male associates who had fewer home responsibilities.

A 1988 study and report by the American Bar Association Commission on Women in the Profession, chaired by Hilary Rodham Clinton, recommended "deep changes in the discriminatory and biased attitudes toward women in the male-defined professional culture."[55] The new corporate women professionals did not appreciate the dominant male value system they encountered there.

When the economic slump worsened in the early nineties, even more pressure was applied at law firms to produce, produce, produce. Many women resigned rather than fight back. They did not feel powerful enough to change the century-old rules that had been made by men. It was also clear to many women that the majority of their male coworkers still believed them incapable of maintaining their "objectivity and rising above emotions."

Many male lawyers claim that motherhood is the main stumbling block to career satisfaction for women attorneys, but the American Bar Association *Journal* reported that 95 percent of women lawyers return to work within a year after a child is born. Furthermore, women in public-sector jobs stay longer than men. The *Journal* conclusion was that women are more demanding of social purpose in their work, . . . more critical of silly professional rituals, and less likely to take to a profession that is built on contention.

Women lawyers have often expressed a deep hatred for the atmosphere at big law firms, where they find "false socializing, tantrums, fraternity style shows of dedication, and murderous competition." And one woman lawyer has noted that "practicing law is antithetical to what most women are brought up to be comfortable with. It's cold, it's hierarchical, it's competitive. More than any other profession I can think of, it has the negative aspects of patriarchy. It runs too much on testosterone and a cultish reverence for aggressiveness."[56]

Many of the brightest and most imaginative of the women in Harrington's study, like their sisters in the 1960s and 1970s, decided to prepare for much lower-paying but more humane work situations. They quickly discovered that public defender law and other noncorporate jobs were looked down on as "the soft stuff," not scholarly or important.

This attitude has had a profound effect on faculty appointments. When colleges are willing and even eager to appoint women faculty members, they want women who have little interest in "the soft stuff." In 1990, only five women were among the sixty-two tenured law professors at Harvard. All but one were white.

An American Bar Association 1990 survey showed similar trends. Almost twice as many women as men were considering changing jobs within the next two years. Another poll questioned 600 female lawyers who had graduated from the classes of 1975 and 1976. When they were asked whether they would have chosen a career in law if they had known the realities, only a little more than half answered yes.[57]

Apparently the same issues that appalled women in law firms were affecting them in law school. On February 10, 1995, *The New York Times* ran an article with the headline, "Men Found to Do Better in Law School than Women." A University of Pennsylvania law school study had found that women were receiving lower grades than men, not only at that institution but at law schools around the nation. In the critical first year of law school, "men were three times as likely as women to be in the top tenth of the class," bringing them law review membership, summer jobs, and law clerkships. The study described the law school experience as "effectively hostile to women" and raised the question of "whether women will get ahead simply by imitating men." The researchers concluded that the few women who went to law school in earlier decades and performed so outstandingly were "an unusually determined group . . . unfazed by discrimination, having experienced it earlier on."

Women law students sent angry letters to the *Times*. One pointed out that professors seldom called on female students and that since "grades are a combination of 'blind' exams and a discretionary 'class participation element,'" this had a profound effect on women's scores. The other letter writer, an NYU law student, pointed out that women "seem more willing to join activities that cater to their interests, or that prepare them for actual legal work, than to pursue grades and honors for their own sake. . . . It may just be we have better things to do."[58]

For some feminists in the 1990s, other problems loomed far larger. Many of the gains of all minorities had been rolled back. Poverty, homelessness, and even hunger had become urgent issues in the United States. One-third of all African Americans and many Latinos had "made it" into the different income layers of the "middle class," but drug addiction, violence, crumbling schools and hospitals, and new and sophisticated forms of racism plagued the inner cities.

Poverty had been increasingly feminized. A 1995 Census report found 46 percent of all African American children living in poverty—three times the percentage of white children. Women and their children made up a larger proportion of the poor than at any other time in United States history.

Women were still ready to fight. They demonstrated that in the mid-1990s, when actions against abortion clinics escalated into firebombings and murders. Thousands of women showed up in Washington, D.C., to show their continued support of the right to choose.

But some women believed that defensive responses were not enough. In 1995 a newly elected Republican majority in Congress was attempting to repeal affirmative action legislation. These women talked about the need for new social movements for the coming twenty-first century. A different kind of organizing effort that would join together all of the forces opposing poverty, racism, and sexism was required to counter attacks on their progress.

In such a movement, women in law could play a critical role if they remembered the opening statement at the Equity Club meeting of women lawyers more than a century earlier: "I believe that as Women Lawyers . . . we must make a special effort . . . for other women besides ourselves."

NOTES

Introduction

1. Quoted in *Current Biography*, February 1994, p. 32.
2. From the 1869 decision of the Illinois Supreme Court denying Myra Bradwell the right to practice law in the state. Quoted in Judith A. Baer, *Women in American Law: The Struggle toward Equality from the New Deal to the Present* (New York: Holmes & Meier,1991), p. 269.
3. Quoted in Baer, p. 269.
4. Alfred Stillé in the 1871 *Transactions of the American Medical Association*. Quoted in Hedda Garza *Women in Medicine* (New York: Franklin Watts, 1994), p. 51.
5. Quoted in Baer, p. 269.
6. David Margolick, "Remaking of the Simpson Prosecutor," *The New York Times*, October 3, 1994, p. A10.

Chapter 1

1. Quoted in Eleanor Flexner, *Century of Struggle: The Woman's Rights Movement in the United States* (Cambridge, Mass.: Belknap Press of Harvard University Press, 1959), p. 47.

2. One woman, Margaret Brent, had acted in a more or less legal capacity in colonial Maryland and two African American women had argued their own cases in court, perhaps because no one would represent them (see Chapter 2). Except where otherwise indicated, most of the facts in this chapter are based on Karen Berger Morello, *The Invisible Bar: The Woman Lawyer in America 1638 to the Present* (New York: Random House, 1986).

3. Before the last decade of the century, almost any one could open a training school for doctors or hang out a shingle and practice medicine. In 1850 the first women's medical college opened in Pennsylvania, despite strong resistance from the state medical society. By then more than 11,000 women had received medical degrees from one or another institution. When more stringent standards were set, most medical colleges maintained strict male-only admission policies. For the full story of women in medicine, see Hedda Garza, *Women in Medicine* (New York: Franklin Watts, 1994).

4. The information on the struggle for women's rights is based on Bettina Aptheker, *Woman's Legacy: Essays on Race, Sex, and Class in American History* (Amherst: University of Massachusetts Press, 1982); Baer; Flexner; Elizabeth H. Pleck and Ellen K. Rothman with Paula Shields, *The Legacies Book* (Washington, D.C.: The Annenberg/CPB Project, 1987); Howard Zinn, *A People's History of the United States* (New York: HarperPerennial, 1990), pp. 102–123.

5. Quoted in Zinn, p. 116.

6. The laws, set down in 1632 in a document called "The Lawes Resolutions of Womens Rights," state that "a woman as soon as she is married is called *covert* . . . that is 'veiled'; as it were, clouded and overshadowed, she hath lost her streame. . . ." When the

American colonies were established, this feudal doctrine of coverture was carried into the new wilderness. The biblical origins of the so-called coverture laws are covered in Leo Kanowitz, *Women and the Law* (Albuquerque: University of New Mexico Press, 1969), p. 35.

7. Aptheker, p. 16.
8. Blackstone set down the marriage rules:

By marriage, the husband and wife are one person in law; that is the very being...of the woman is suspended during the marriage, or at least is incorporated and consolidated.

—Blackstone Commentaries, p. 443.
Quoted in Kanowitz, p. 35.

9. See David F. Noble. *A World Without Women* (New York: Alfred A. Knopf, 1992), pp. 208–209.
10. Quoted in Garza, p. 20. Over the course of more than 200 years after 1479, estimates run as high as 9 million people tortured and executed as witches throughout Europe. Women victims outnumbered male victims by as high as ten to one in many places. Even in the American colonies, nineteen women were executed by hanging in Salem, Massachusetts, in 1696 when they would not confess to witchcraft.
11. Quoted in Kanowitz, p. 37.
12. Quoted in Zinn, p. 109.
13. This seldom reported response is cited by Judith A. Baer, *Women in American Law: The Struggle toward Equality from the New Deal to the Present* (New York: Holmes & Meier, 1991), p. 19.
14. Quoted in Flexner, pp. 14–15.
15. Colonial poverty is covered by Zinn on pp. 50–53.
16. Quoted in Zinn, p. 108.
17. She wrote in part: "Will it be said that the judgment of a male two years old, is more sage than that of a

female's of the same age? I believe the reverse is generally observed to be true. But from that period what partiality! How is the one exalted and the other depressed, by the contrary modes of education that are adopted! The one is taught to aspire, the other is early confined and limited. As their years increase, the sister must be wholly domesticated, while the brother is led by the hand through all the flowery paths of science." Quoted in Flexner, p. 16.

Two years later, the better-known *Vindication of the Rights of Women* by Mary Wollstonecraft appeared in England. This book's appearance usually is considered the opening gun of the modern women's rights movement. The two books circulated around the United States around the same time. Wollstonecraft's work was in answer to Edmund Burke, an Englishman who took the myth of female inferiority to a new level, writing that "a woman is but an animal, and an animal not of the highest order." Wollstonecraft urged women "to acquire strength, both of mind and body . . . and that those beings who are only the objects of pity and that kind of love . . . will soon become objects of contempt . . ." Quoted in Zinn, p. 110.

18. Hannah Mather Crocker, for example, author of *Observations on the Real Rights of Women* in 1818, supported the educational advancement of women but added words that undoubtedly pleased the male legal establishment:

It would be morally wrong, and physically imprudent, for any woman to attempt pleading at the bar of justice, as no law can give her right of deviating from the strictest rules of rectitude and decorum.

—Quoted in Flexner, p. 24.

19. Quoted in Zinn, pp. 116–117.
20. She warned that "until women assume the place in society which good sense and good feeling alike assign to them, human improvement must advance but feebly . . . Until power is annihilated on one side, fear and obedience on the other, and both restored to their birthright—equality." Quoted in Zinn, p. 120.
21. Quoted in Flexner, p. 29.
22. Ibid., p. 30.
23. See Flexner, p. 342, note 13.
24. Quoted in Flexner, p. 58.
25. Ibid., p. 42.
26. He said "When the true history of the antislavery cause shall be written, women will occupy a large space in its pages, for the cause of the slave had been peculiarly woman's cause. . . . Her skill, industry, patience and perseverance have been wonderfully manifest in every trial hour. Not only did her feet run on"willing errands," and her fingers do the work which in large degree supplied the sinews of war, but her deep moral convictions, and her tender human sensibilities found convincing and persuasive expression in her pen and her voice." Quoted in Aptheker, p. 15.
27. Quoted in Flexner, p. 47.
28. Ibid, p. 48.
29. In 1837, a pastoral letter from the Council of Congregationalist Ministers of Massachusetts, ranted against the unwomanly and un-Christian behavior of antislavery women. Quoted in Flexner, p. 46.
30. Quoted in Flexner, p. 51.
31. For details of this little-known story, see Aptheker, pp. 29–30.
32. Quoted in Zinn, p. 122.

Chapter 2

1. Quoted in Jane M. Friedman. *America's First Woman Lawyer: The Biography of Myra Bradwell*. (Buffalo,

N.Y.: Prometheus Books, 1993), p. 17. Much of the information on Myra Bradwell in this and subsequent chapters is based on Friedman's pathbreaking biography.

2. Governor Calvert returned to England in 1643, leaving Margaret Brent as his appointed counsel. Brent put down a rebellion against Calvert during his absence, promising payment to the hired soldiers. Calvert died soon after he returned, but he assigned Brent the job of settling his accounts and the court formally recognized her as the "administrator of Leonard Calvert." She believed she had the right as attorney for the governor to have "vote and voyce" in the Maryland Assembly, but none of the legislators would go that far. Gaining the reputation of a most able lawyer, she represented Calvert's estate in court and pressed legal action against his debtors in order to pay his defending army. Charges against Brent were sent to the Maryland Assembly by angry debtors, but the assembly refused to move against Brent, instead complimenting her for keeping the peace. There can be little doubt of Margaret Brent's capability and courage, but there is no evidence that she said or did anything to improve the lowly legal status of other colonial women. For more on the life of Brent, see Karen Berger Morello, *The Invisible Bar: The Woman Lawyer in America 1638 to the Present* (New York: Random House, 1986), pp. 4–8.

3. Quoted in Friedman, p. 78.

4. She had been admitted during the last years of the Civil War, when enrollments of men were at rockbottom.

5. She became a well-known lecturer on women's rights, and later she and her husband joined the faculty at DePauw University in Indiana.

6. Quoted in Friedman, p. 133.

7. Quoted in Morello, p. 132.

8. Quoted in Friedman, p. 132.

9. Ibid., p. 133.

10. Sources for this section on the women's rights movement are Bettina Aptheker, *Woman's Legacy* (Amherst: University of Massachusetts Press, 1982); Angela Y. Davis, *Women, Race & Class* (New York: Vintage Books, 1983); and Eleanor Flexner, *Century of Struggle* (Cambridge, Mass.: Harvard University Press, 1959).
11. Quoted in Flexner, p. 144.
12. Frederick Douglass rose to make an angry speech in response:

    When women because they are women, are dragged from their homes and hung upon lamp-posts; when their children are torn from their arms and their brains dashed out upon the pavement . . . when they are in danger of having their homes burnt down over their heads; when their children are not allowed to enter schools; they will have an urgency to obtain the ballot.

    Someone in the audience yelled out, "Is that not all true about black women?" Douglass replied: "Yes, yes, yes, it is true of the black woman, but not because she is a woman but because she is black."

    —Quoted in Aptheker, pp. 47–48.

13. Details of Bradwell's reaction to the events are recounted in Friedman, pp. 168–173.
14. Quoted in Morello, p. 71.
15. Ibid., pp. 31–32.
16. Ibid., p. 34.
17. States' rights provisions in the U.S. Constitution became a real barrier to voting rights for minorities and legal rights and suffrage for women for more than a century. As long as no constitutional amendment prohibited it, individual states could pass and enforce legislation that blocked progress.
18. Quoted in Friedman, p. 144.
19. Quoted in Morello, p. 25.
20. Quoted in Friedman, p. 135.

21. Quoted in Morello, pp. 173–174.
22. The quotations are from Friedman, who, despite the deliberate destruction of much of the correspondence involved in the case, was able to dig out the facts. (pp. 47–69)
23. Mrs. Lincoln wrote: "When all others, among them my husband's supposed friends, failed me in the most bitter hours of my life, these loyal hearts, Myra and James Bradwell, came to my assistance and rescued me under great difficulty from confinement in an insane asylum." Quoted in Friedman, p. 51.
24. Quoted in Friedman, p. 102.
25. Ibid., p. 103.
26. Ibid., p. 130.
27. Quoted in Morello, pp. 90–91.
28. Ibid., p. 67.
29. Ibid., p. 68.
30. Ibid., p. 47.
31. Ibid., p. 47.
32. Ibid., p. 48.
33. Quoted in Friedman, p. 131.
34. The story of Clara Foltz is based on Mortimer D. Schwartz, Susan L. Brandt, and Patience Milrod, "The Battles of Clara Shortridge Foltz," *California Defender*, Spring 1985, vol. 1, no. 1, pp. 7–13; Morello, pp. 54–55; and Friedman, pp. 131–132,
35. Quoted in Morello, p. 59.
36. During a rancorous debate, Foltz later described that "narrow-gauge statesmen grew as red as turkey gobblers. . . ." The state legislators were willing to eliminate the word *white* but strongly opposed removing the word *male*. Opponents presented the same old arguments, many of them sprinkling the sugar of flattery onto the vinegar of their contempt. Women's sphere "was infinitely more important than that of men, and that sphere was the home." Women were far too "delicate" to hear the "indelicate evidence" heard in many courtrooms.

One supporter reminded his fellow legislators that women had been officially licensed to practice medicine since 1867. Clearly they were not too "delicate" to deal with illness and corpses. The bill nevertheless was defeated by a three-vote margin, but its supporters managed to pass a bill to reconsider the next day. Foltz worked the corridors of the legislature all night, finally winning by two votes. Women in California would be admitted to the bar.

37. Quoted in Morello, p. 62.
38. Ibid., p. 64.
39. Quoted in Friedman, p. 129.
40. In October 1874, a unanimous Supreme Court decision brought a major defeat for the suffrage movement. Two years earlier, Virginia Minor, the president of the Missouri Woman Suffrage Association, attempted to register to vote in Missouri and was turned away. Minor and her lawyer husband, Francis Minor, filed a suit that finally made its way to the U.S. Supreme Court. They based their appeal on the rights of citizens as outlined in the Fourteenth Amendment and lost their case. The Minor decision made it clear that voting laws were to be decided by the states. See Karen DeCrow, *Sexist Justice* (New York: Random House, 1974), pp. 18–20.

Chapter 3

1. Quoted in Karen Berger Morello, *The Invisible Bar* (New York: Random House, 1986), p. 83.
2. Sources of information in this chapter were Bettina Aptheker, *Woman's Legacy: Essays on Race, Sex, and Class in American History* (Amherst: University of Massachusetts Press, 1982); Angela Y. Davis, *Women, Race & Class* (New York: Vintage Books, 1983); Cynthia Fuchs Epstein, *Women in Law* (New York: Basic Books, 1981); Eleanor Flexner, *Century*

of Struggle (Cambridge, Mass.: Belknap Press of Harvard University Press, 1970); and Karen Berger Morello, *The Invisible Bar* (New York: Random House), 1986.

3. For details see Hedda Garza, *Women in Medicine,* (New York: Franklin Watts, 1994), pp. 53–56.
4. By the turn of the century, about 115 black women were practicing physicians, about half of them graduating from black medical schools. Four African American women became the first of any race to pass the state licensing examinations in four southern states. See Garza, *Women in Medicine*, p. 87.
5. See James D. Cockcroft, *The Hispanic Struggle for Social Justice* (New York: Franklin Watts, 1994).
6. Quoted in Flexner, p. 99.
7. See Aptheker, pp. 107–108.
8. The best source for biographical information on African-American women is Jessie Carney Smith, ed., *Notable Black American Women* (Detroit: Gale Research, 1992). The biographies are arranged alphabetically.
9. For more on this little-discussed collaboration, see Davis, pp. 98–109.
10. Quoted in Smith, p. 922.
11. Quoted in Flexner, p. 128.
12. Ibid., p. 128.
13. Quoted in Morello, p. 144.
14. Quotes are from Jane M. Friedman, *America's First Woman Lawyer: The Biography of Myra Bradwell* (Buffalo, N.Y.: Prometheus Books, 1993), p. 132.
15. For details see Flexner, pp. 188–192, and Davis, pp. 127–136.
16. Quoted in Morello, p. 54.
17. For details, see Mortimer D. Schwartz, Susan L. Brandt, and Patience Milrod. "The Battles of Clara Shortridge Foltz." *California Defender*, Spring 1985, Vol. 1, Issue 1, pp. 7-13.

18. Quotes are from Schwartz, Brandt, and Milrod, p. 10.
19. Quoted in Morello, p. 177.
20. Quoted in Flexner, p. 161.
21. Quoted in Friedman, p. 177.
22. Quoted in Flexner, p. 138.
23. Quotes are from Morello, pp. 90-91.
24. Ibid., pp. 120, 121.
25. Quoted in Morello, p. 121.
26. For further information, see Mary V. Dearborn, *Love in the Promised Land* (New York: The Free Press, 1988), pp. 45–47.
27. They included J. Ellen Foster, of Iowa; Ada H. Kepley, the first woman law graduate in the nation, who published a newspaper in Illinois listing the names of men frequenting saloons in the area; Lavinia Goodell, Wisconsin's first woman lawyer; and Nebraska's first, Ada Bittenbinder, who became the attorney for WCTU in 1888 and ran for a state Supreme Court judgeship on the Prohibition Party ticket in 1891.
28. Quoted in Morello, p. 79.
29. Ibid., pp. 80–81.
30. Others at the Women's Legal Education Society said that Dr. Kempin left because of the rude treatment she received from the students at the University of New York, as well as the impossibility of receiving a full-time appointment. See Morello, pp. 79–80.
31. It was later said of her that "whatever claims may be made as to the exact brain in which the idea of equal pay was born, it is undisputed that Kate Hogan brought before the people of the state sex discrimination in the salary schedules of the Board of Education and sent the slogan 'Equal Pay for Equal Work' thundering round the world." Quoted in Morello, p. 82.
32. For details, see Davis, p. 131.
33. Quoted in Morello, p. 83.
34. Ibid., p. 42.

Chapter 4

1. Quoted in Karen Berger Morello, *The Invisible Bar* (New York: Random House, 1986), p. 126.
2. Quoted in Morello, p. 176.
3. According to both U.S. Bureau of the Census data and *Law Directory* figures, even in 1963, women lawyers were estimated at 2.7 to 3.3 percent of the lawyers in the United States, with growth remaining just about static from 1910 to 1960. See tables in Cynthia Fuchs Epstein, *Women in Law* (New York: Basic Books, 1981), p. 4.
4. The story and quotes are adapted from Morello, pp. 125–127.
5. Details on women lawyers during the presuffrage and early postsuffrage periods can be found in Morello; and Ronald Chester, *Unequal Access* (South Hadley, Mass.: Bergin & Garvey Publishers, 1985).
6. MacLean's law partner founded a similar school for men, later called Suffolk Law School. Washington College of Law was open to men and women from its founding days. In 1914, twenty-five men and twenty women graduated. The history of Portia and Suffolk law schools is covered by Chester.
7. For more on this see Hedda Garza, *Women in Medicine* (New York: Franklin Watts, 1994).
8. Quotes are in Morello, pp. 175–76.
9. Quoted in Morello, p. 180.
10. On one occasion at a public meeting Rose Schnei derman was asked by a New York state senator whether women would become less feminine if they went to the polls. Schneiderman did not mince words when she replied:

    We have women working in the foundries, stripped to the waist, if you please, because of the heat. Yet the Senator says nothing about these women losing their charms. They have got to retain their charm and delicacy and

*work in the foundries. Of course you know the reason
they are employed in foundries is that they are cheaper
and work longer hours than men. Women in the laundries, for instance, stand for thirteen and fourteen hours
in the terrible steam and heat with their hands in hot
starch. Surely these women won't lose any more of their
beauty and charm by putting a ballot in a ballot box once
a year than they are likely to lose standing in foundries
or laundries all year round. There is no harder contest
than the contest for bread, let me tell you that.*

—Quoted in Eleanor Flexner, *Century of Struggle:
The Women's Rights Movement in the United States*
(Cambridge, Mass.: Belknap Press of Harvard
University Press, 1959), pp. 258–259.

11. Quoted in Morello, p. 129.
12. For details, see Morello, pp. 142–172.
13. Quoted in Morello, pp. 147–148.
14. Quoted in Flexner, p. 281.
15. For the story of African Americans in World War I, see Hedda Garza, *African Americans and Jewish Americans* (New York: Franklin Watts, 1995), Chapter 3.
16. For details, see Flexner, pp. 283–287.
17. These included Ohio, Indiana, Rhode Island, Nebraska, and Michigan. Arkansas broke the solid southern block against suffrage on March 6, but the women lost a referendum in Maine. They geared up for the most important wartime referendum, New York State. In New York City right before the vote, powerful Tammany Hall politicians, the greatest stumbling block to women's suffrage, announced that they would not oppose the referendum. Many of the politicians had female relatives working in the Woman Suffrage Party or NAWSA. Suffrage won by a margin of 100,000 in New York City, with just about a fifty-fifty split vote in the rest of the state.
18. For details, see Flexner, p. 302.
19. Quoted in Garza, *African Americans and Jewish Americans*, p. 118.

20. Quoted in Stuart Ewen, *Captains of Consciousness* (New York: McGraw-Hill, 1976), p. 161.
21. Quoted in Ewen, p. 160.
22. Ibid., p. 161.
23. In 1924, 82 percent of Portia graduates passed the bar examination. As the tests became more difficult, by 1929, 65 percent of Portia's women passed compared to the overall pass rate of 40 percent. In 1932, only 130 out of 693 applicants for the bar examination passed the test on the first try. An amazing 91 of them had studied at part-time schools. Ten women from Portia and six other women passed. See Chester, p. 10.
24. This and subsequent sections on poverty law are based on Martha F. Davis, *Brutal Need: Lawyers and the Welfare Rights Movement, 1960–1973* (New Haven, Conn.: Yale University Press, 1993), and Marlise James, *The People's Lawyers* (New York: Holt, Rinehart and Winston, 1973).
25. Using language that was heard again and again in future decades, President Roosevelt insisted that "continued dependence upon relief induces a spiritual and moral disintegration fundamentally destructive to the national fiber. . . ." Quoted in Davis, p. 7.
26. Quoted in Davis, p. 16. The American Bar Association, instead of urging its members to take on some poor clients, stepped up its support for Legal Aid societies. The number of cases handled by Legal Aid societies rose from 96,000 annually in 1920 to almost 172,000 in 1929.
27. Quoted in Davis, p. 17.
28. Quotes are from Morello, p. 85.
29. Quoted in Morello, p. 187.
30. See Morello, p. 226.
31. Quoted in Morello, p. 96.
32. Ibid., p. 97.
33. Sources for information on black women attorneys are Morello; Jessie Carney Smith, ed., *Notable Black*

American Women (Detroit: Gale Research, 1992), with biographies arranged alphabetically.

34. For details, see James D. Cockcroft, *The Hispanic Struggle for Social Justice* (New York: Franklin Watts, 1994).

35. For details on Latinas in the professions, see Hedda Garza, *Latinas* (New York: Franklin Watts, 1994), pp. 131–162; and Diane Telgen and Jim Kamp, eds., *Notable Hispanic Women* (Detroit: Gale Research, 1993), with biographies arranged alphabetically.

36. Quoted in Morello, p. 149.

37. For details, see Smith, pp. 165–166.

38. See Smith, p. 94.

Chapter Five

1. Quoted in Alan Covey, ed., *A Century of Women* (Atlanta: Turner Publishing, 1994), p. 52.

2. Quoted in Karen DeCrow, *Sexist Justice* (New York: Random House, 1974), p. 108.

3. The proportion of women in the law profession rose from 2.1 to 2.4 percent from 1930 to 1940 and then to 3.5 percent by 1950, declining again to 3.3 percent by 1960. Source is Cynthia Fuchs Epstein, *Women in Law* (New York: Basic Books, 1981), table on p. 4.

4. Sources for this chapter unless otherwise noted are Judith A. Baer, *Women in American Law: The Struggle toward Equality from the New Deal to the Present* (New York: Holmes & Meier, 1991), pp. 269–275; Covey; Karen DeCrow, *Sexist Justice* (New York: Random House, 1974); Leo Kanowitz, *Women and the Law: The Unfinished Revolution* (Albuquerque: University of New Mexico Press, 1969,) pp. 100–148; and Karen Berger Morello, *The Invisible Bar* (New York: Random House), 1986.

5. Quoted in Hedda Garza, *Women in Medicine* (New York: Franklin Watts, 1994), p. 75.

6. Quoted in Kanowitz, p. 34.

7. For details see Marlise James, *The People's Lawyers* (New York: Holt, Rinehart and Winston, 1973), pp. 88–96.

8. Quoted in James, p. 91.

9. Quoted in Epstein, p. 239.

10. The Barbie story is told in James D. Cockcroft, *Latin America*, 2nd ed. (Chicago: Nelson-Hall, 1995), p. 503.

11. Quoted in James, p. xvi.

12. Ibid., p. 91.

13. For details, see Martha F. Davis, *Brutal Need: Lawyers and the Welfare Rights Movement, 1960–1973* (New Haven, Conn.: Yale University Press, 1993), p. 19.

14. For details, see Baer, pp. 209–241.

15. Quotes are from Morello, pp. 101–104.

16. Quoted in Jill Abramson and Barbara Franklin, *Where They Are Now: The Story of the Women of Harvard Law 1974* (Garden City, N.Y.: Doubleday, 1986), p. 12.

17. Quotes from Ruth Bader Ginsburg are in Lynn Gilbert and Gaylen Moore, *Particular Passions* (New York: Clarkson N. Potter, 1981), pp. 167–169.

18. Quoted in *Current Biography*, 1982, p. 298.

19. See also Morello, p. 218.

20. Quoted in Morello, p. 103.

21. Quoted in Baer, p. 215

22. Mona Harrington, *Women Lawyers: Rewriting the Rules* (New York: Alfred A. Knopf, 1994), p. 12.

23. For details, see Kanowitz, p. 29–30.

24. For more on Vidal Santaella, see Diane Telgen and Jim Kamp, eds., *Notable Hispanic American Women* (Detroit: Gale Research, 1993), pp. 369–371.

25. Quoted in Morello, p. 154.

26. The principle sources of information on civil rights during the post–World War II period are Donald McCoy and Richard T. Ruetten, *Quest and Response: Minority Rights and the Truman Administration*

(Wichita: University Press of Kansas, 1973); and Howard Zinn, A *People's History of the United States* (New York: HarperPerennial, 1980), pp. 409–434.

27. For the full story of this effort, see Hedda Garza, *African Americans and Jewish Americans* (New York: Franklin Watts, 1995), Chapter 5; and James D. Cockcroft, *The Hispanic Struggle for Social Justice* (New York: Franklin Watts, 1994).
28. Quoted in McCoy and Ruetten, p. 48.
29. Quoted in Zinn, p. 440.
30. The information on black women lawyers is based on Morello, pp. 173–193; and Jessie Carney Smith ed., *Notable Black American Women* (Detroit: Gale Research, 1992).
31. Quoted in Morello, p. 156.
32. For details on Motley, see Gilbert and Moore, pp. 136–141; and Smith, pp. 779–781.
33. Quoted in Smith, p. 970.
34. There are dozens of excellent books on the Civil Rights Movement, including Dorothy Sterling, *Tear Down the Walls!* (Garden City: Doubleday, 1968); Emma Gelders Sterne, *I Have a Dream* (New York: Alfred A. Knopf, 1965); Langston Hughes and Milton Meltzer, *African American History* (New York: Scholastic, 1990).
35. Quoted in Covey, p. 50.
36. Quoted in Kanowitz, p. 102.
37. Baer, pp. 52–116, thoroughly covers the issue of laws relating to working women.
38. Details on the struggle for passage of the Civil Rights Act of 1964 can be found in DeCrow, pp. 105–107; and Kanowitz, pp. 100–106.
39. Quoted in Kanowitz, pp. 104–105.
40. Quoted in DeCrow, p. 106.
41. Quotes are from Covey, p. 52.
42. Quoted in DeCrow, p. 108.
43. Ibid., p. 108.

44. Quoted in Covey, p. 52.
45. For details, see Covey, p. 53.

Chapter 6

1. Quoted in Judith A. Baer, *Women in American Law: The Struggle toward Equality from the New Deal to the Present* (Holmes & Meier, 1991), p. 167.
2. Quoted in Karen Berger Morello, *The Invisible Bar* (New York: Random House, 1986), p. 189.
3. Quoted in Catharine A. MacKinnon, *Feminism Unmodified* (Cambridge, Mass.: Harvard University Press, 1987), pp. 70–71.
4. Much of the information in this chapter was based on Baer; Mona Harrington, *Women Lawyers: Rewriting the Rules* (New York: Alfred A. Knopf, 1994); Marlise James, *The People's Lawyers* (New York: Holt, Rinehart and Winston, 1973); and Morello.
5. At the 1965 convention of the leading student organization, Students for a Democratic Society, for example, a group of women pressed for a statement on women's liberation and were ridiculed and expelled from the meeting hall. Four years later, during a demonstration against the Vietnam War at President Richard Nixon's inauguration, one woman speaker made remarks favoring women's equality and was greeted with catcalls and crude sexist insults from her "co-thinkers." Even in the Latino movement, where Dolores Huerta had gained national respect for her role in the United Farm Workers, a new organization called La Raza Unida presented a multi-issue platform covering racism, employment issues, farmworkers' rights, and an end to the Vietnam war, but prohibited the discussion of women's rights. For more details, see Hedda Garza, *Latinas* (New York: Franklin Watts, 1994), pp. 111–114.

6. For details, see James, pp. 93–96.
7. Quoted in James, p. 274.
8. NWRO also conducted an educational campaign to counter the stereotyped portrayals of welfare mothers as cheaters and liars. NWRO publicized the fact that most welfare recipients in the nation were elderly, disabled, or blind. More than half were children and only 13 percent were the mothers of small children. Many of them were the working poor, full-time hospital workers, domestics who were paid so little they qualified for aid! Basically this permitted their employers to continue paying them minimum wage salaries.
9. For more information, see Cynthia Fuchs Epstein, *Women in Law* (New York: Basic Books, 1981), pp. 141–150.
10. Quoted in James, pp. 116–117.
11. For details, see Morello, pp. 103–104.
12. The section on Hillary Rodham Clinton is based on Judith Warner, *Hillary Clinton: The Inside Story* (New York: Signet, 1993); and Donnie Radcliffe, *Hillary Rodham Clinton* (New York: Warner Books, 1993).
13. Quoted in Lynne Gilbert and Gaylen Moore, *Particular Passions* (New York: Clarkson N. Potter, Inc., 1981), p. 186.
14. This section is based on Jill Abramson and Barbara Franklin, *Where They Are Now: The Story of the Women of Harvard Law 1974* (Garden City, N.Y.: Doubleday, 1986).
15. Quoted in Abramson and Franklin, p. 123.
16. For details, see Sarah Weddington, *A Question of Choice* (New York: G.P. Putnam's Sons, 1992).
17. Quoted in Weddington, p. 11.
18. Ibid., p. 70.
19. In Georgia, Margie Pitts Hames, a volunteer for the ACLU, was in court with *Doe* v. *Bolton*. In Min-

neapolis, a woman doctor was appealing her 1970 conviction for performing an abortion on a woman who had German measles and feared that her baby had been damaged.

20. For more on the ERA, see Baer, p. 127.
21. Actually, the pregnancy rate is about the same no matter what the circumstances of sexual intercourse—about 4 percent. See Baer, pp. 203–204.
22. Quoted in Baer, p. 203.
23. Quoted in Hunter College, *Women's Realities, Women's Choices* (New York: Oxford University Press, 1995), p. 427.
24. Excerpted from Hunter College, p. 428.
25. Quoted in Harrington, p. 177.
26. Quoted in "Gender Bias in the Judicial System," in *Wildfire*, vol. 6, no. 4, Fall/Winter 1994, p. 25.
27. See Harrington, p. 179.
28. Quotes are from James, pp. 282–287.
29. Quoted in Gilbert and Moore, p. 144.
30. Quoted in Morello, p. 172.
31. For details on Latina attorneys, see Nicolas Kanellos, ed., *The Hispanic American Almanac* (Detroit: Gale Research, 1993), pp. 238–241.
32. See in Diana Telgen and Jim Kamp, eds., *Notable Hispanic American Women* (Detroit: Gale Research Inc., 1993), p. 197. Unless otherwise stated, all subsequent biographical sketches and quotations from individual Latinas may be located in alphabetical order in Telgen and Kamp. See also Garza, *Latinas*.
33. *New York Times*, December 2, 1993 p. B2.
34. In 1978 only eight states had more than 4 percent of women attorneys actively engaged in litigation practices. For more information, see Paul B. Wice, *Criminal Lawyers: An Endangered Species* (Beverly Hills, Calif.: Sage Publications, 1978).
35. Quoted in Wice, p. 68.
36. Quoted in Morello, p. 175.

37. Ibid., p. 189.
38. Quotes are from Morello, pp. 192–193.
39. Quoted in Morello, pp. 270–271.
40. Ibid., p. 245.
41. Ibid., p. 245.
42. Although by 1983, 13 percent of lawyers were women, only 5 percent were state appellate judges and 2 percent state trial judges; and on the federal bench, 11 percent sat on the court of appeals and only 6.9 percent on district courts. In 1969, Shirley Hofstedler was the only woman serving on the U.S. Court of Appeals since Florence Ellinwood Allen was appointed to that position. Only three women, Sarah Hughes, Constance Baker Motley, and June L. Green, served on the federal district court. As late as 1977, Cornelia G. Kennedy, Sixth Circuit Court of Appeals judge, commented about the rarity of women judges. Data for this section on woman judges are from Morello, pp. 218–223.
43. Quoted in Morello, p. 218.
44. Quoted in Jane M. Friedman, *America's First Woman Lawyer: The Biography of Myra Bradwell* (Buffalo, N.Y.: Prometheus Books, 1993), p. 212.
45. See Susan Faludi, *Backlash* (New York: Crown Publishers, 1991).
46. U.S. Department of Commerce, Bureau of the Census, "Equal Employment Opportunity File," 1990. (Unpublished but issued in 1993 on CD-ROM only.)
47. For background and details, see James D. Cockcroft, *Hispanics in the Struggle for Equal Education* (New York: Franklin Watts, 1995); and Kanellos, p. 356.
48. There were almost 4,000 "Asian and Pacific Islanders" women in the legal profession in 1990 and almost 7,000 men.
49. See "The Truth about Women's Wages," in *Working Woman*, April 1993.

50. David Gates, "White Male Paranoia," *Newsweek*, March 29, 1993, pp. 48–53.
51. Quoted in Catharine A. MacKinnon, *Feminism Unmodified* (Cambridge, Mass.: Harvard University Press, 1987), pp. 70–71.
52. Quoted in Harrington, p. 10.
53. Quoted in Laura Mansnerus, "Why Woman Are Leaving the Law," in *Working Woman*, April 1993, p. 65.
54. Quotes are from Harrington, p. 62.
55. Between 1986 and 1991, about 1,000 people, again more women than men, had left their nine midsize and large Manhattan firms. Twenty-one percent of the men had achieved partnership status compared with 8 percent of the women. For details, see Mansnerus, p. 65.
56. *New York Times*, February 17, 1995.
57. CBS "Evening News," February 23, 1995.
58. Quoted in Morello, p. 54.

SUGGESTED READING

BOOKS

Books especially recommended for students are marked with an asterisk (*).

*Abramson, Jill, and Barbara Franklin. *Where They Are Now: The Story of the Women of Harvard Law 1974.* Garden City, N.Y.: Doubleday, 1986.

Aptheker, Bettina. *Woman's Legacy: Essays on Race, Sex, and Class in American History.* Amherst: University of Massachusetts Press, 1982.

Baer, Judith A. *Women in American Law: The Struggle toward Equality from the New Deal to the Present.* New York: Holmes & Meier, 1991.

Chester, Ronald. *Unequal Access.* South Hadley, Mass.: Bergin & Garvey Publishers, 1985.

*Cockcroft, James D. *Hispanics in the Struggle for Equal Education.* New York: Franklin Watts, 1995.

*Cockcroft, James D. *The Hispanic Struggle for Social Justice.* New York: Franklin Watts, 1994.

*Covey, Alan, ed. *A Century of Women*. Atlanta: Turner Publishing, 1994.

Davis, Angela Y. *Women, Race & Class*. New York: Vintage Books, 1983.

Davis, Martha F., *Brutal Need: Lawyers and the Welfare Rights Movement, 1960–1973*. New Haven: Yale University Press, 1993.

DeCrow, Karen. *Sexist Justice*. New York: Random House, 1974.

Epstein, Cynthia Fuchs. *Women in Law*. New York: Basic Books, 1981.

Faludi, Susan. *Backlash*. New York: Crown Publishers, 1991.

*Flexner, Eleanor. *Century of Struggle: The Women's Rights Movement in the United States*. Cambridge, Mass.: Balknap Press of Harvard University Press, 1959.

*Friedman, Jane M. *America's First Woman Lawyer: The Biography of Myra Bradwell*. Buffalo, N.Y.: Prometheus Books, 1993.

*Garza, Hedda. *Latinas: Hispanic Women in the United States*. New York: Franklin Watts, 1994.

*Garza, Hedda. *Women in Medicine*. New York: Franklin Watts, 1994.

*Gilbert, Lynn, and Gaylen Moore. *Particular Passions*. New York: Clarkson N. Potter, 1981.

Harrington, Mona. *Women Lawyers: Rewriting the Rules*. New York: Alfred A. Knopf, 1994.

*Kanellos, Nicolas, ed. *The Hispanic-American Almanac.* Detroit: Gale Research, 1993.

Hunter College. *Women's Realities, Women's Choices.* New York: Oxford University Press, 1995.

*James, Marlise. *The People's Lawyers.* New York: Holt, Rinehart and Winston, 1973.

Kanowitz, Leo. *Women and the Law: The Unfinished Revolution.* Albuquerque: University of New Mexico Press, 1969.

MacKinnon, Catharine A. *Feminism Unmodified.* Cambridge, Mass.: Harvard University Press, 1987.

*Morello, Karen Berger. *The Invisible Bar: The Woman Lawyer in America 1638 to the Present.* New York: Random House, 1986.

*Pleck, Elizabeth H., and Ellen K. Rothman, with Paula Shields *The Legacies Book.* Washington, D.C.: The Annenberg/CPB Project, 1987.

*Smith, Jessie Carney, ed. *Notable Black American Women.* Detroit: Gale Research, 1992.

*Sterling, Dorothy. *Tear Down the Walls! A History of the American Civil Rights Movement.* Garden City, N.Y.: Doubleday, 1968.

*Telgen, Diane, and Jim Kamp, eds. *Notable Hispanic American Women.* Detroit: Gale Research, 1993.

*Warner, Judith. *Hillary Clinton: The Inside Story.* New York: Signet, 1993.

*Weddington, Sarah. *A Question of Choice*. New York: G.P. Putnam's Sons, 1992.

Wice, Paul B. *Criminal Lawyers: An Endangered Species*. Beverly Hills, Calif.: Sage Publications, 1978.

*Zinn, Howard. *A People's History of the United States*. New York: HarperPerennial, 1990.

JOURNALS

California Defender

Working Woman

INDEX

219

221

Ricker, Marilla Young, 71, 77
Robinson, Jackie, 136
Robinson, Lelia J., 53–54, 73
Roe v. Wade, 112, 166–67
Rogers, Nathaniel P., 30
Roosevelt, Franklin D., 104–5, 109
Roosevelt, Franklin D., Jr., 149
Root, Gladys Towles, 107–8
Rose, Ernestine, 29
Rush, Gertrude E., 94
Ryan, Edward, 45–47

St. Louis Law School, 37, 108
Sampson, Edith S., 115, 140
Santanella, Irma Vidal, 123, 134, 176
Schneiderman, Rose, 89
Schofield, Emma Fall, 103
Schroeder, Patricia, 127
Schweiger, Clara, 88
Schwerner, Michael "Mickey," 148, 149
Schwerner, Rita, 148
Seidenberg, Faith, 157
Shapiro, Robert L., 13
Sharp, Susie M., 180
Silver, Carol Ruth, 156
Simonson, Archie, 182
Slavitt, Charlotte, 103–4

Smith, Lena O., 113
Smith, Reginald Heber, 105
Southworth, Anne C., 47–48
Springer, Francis, 36
Spyri, Emily Kempin, 78, 79
Stanton, Elizabeth Cady, 30, 40–42, 89
Still, Letetia, 26
Stillé, Alfred, 11, 12
Stone, Harlan Fiske, 105–6, 111
Stone, Lucy, 22, 24, 41, 58
Stow, Marietta, 77
Stowe, Harriet Beecher, 63
Strickland, Martha, 70
Strong, George Templeton, 50, 52
Strong, Theon G., 83
Sullivan, Marian, 134

Taylor, Anna Deggs, 147–48
Thomas, Clarence, 171
Till, Emmett, 141
Titus, Melle Stanleyetta, 79–80
Truman, Harry S., 122, 135–36, 140
Turner, Nat, 25

University of Chicago Law School, 37, 65